Praise for *Lead with Hospitality*

"This is the secret sauce leaders need to elevate their game! During a time of uncertainty and unpredictability, Taylor Scott gives his readers actionable steps that executives can start today. This will be a game changer read, especially for leaders who are working remotely and want to find ways to better connect to their teams."

—Laura Cazatt, senior manager of brand merchandising at the Walt Disney Company

"Connecting with people on a human level opens up the pathway to leading them to become their best. Taylor Scott paints a perfect picture of the threads between gracious hospitality and transformational leadership. This book is as educational as it is entertaining, and as useful as it is inspiring."

—Chip Conley, strategic advisor for hospitality and leadership at Airbnb and founder of Modern Elder Academy

"The fundamentals of hospitality are not preserved only for the guests to experience. Instead, Taylor proves that authentically connecting with your employees, treating them with those same hospitable guiding principles, is what elevates leaders to greatness. By sharing his own personal experiences working with some of the hospitality greats, he lays out a plan that is not only actionable, but enjoyable. Now more than ever, our ability to create meaningful connections with our employees is paramount. If you lead people, you need this book!"

—Sarah Moore, vice president of brand marketing at MGM Resorts International

"This book gets to the heart of what matters (or should) in organizations today. Taylor Scott has worked for some blue chip organizations and he's taken what he learned from experience and now teaches how these ideas will make your business better."

—Mark Sanborn, president of Sanborn & Associates, Inc. and author of *The Fred Factor* and *The Intention Imperative*

"Taylor walks the walk! His ability to create genuine connections with his peers and teams is almost magical. I've worked alongside Taylor and experienced his passion and success in creating a culture of learning where people feel seen and heard."

—Colleen Birch, senior vice president of revenue optimization at The Cosmopolitan of Las Vegas

"Taylor Scott's stories illustrate the power of leading with hospitality and his action plans offer step by step guides to setting yourself apart as a transformational leader. You can read this book today and be better tomorrow."

—Joni Teragawachi, director of global learning design at United Airlines

"Moving into 2021 and understanding the changes in the world of hospitality, *Lead with Hospitality* is a book all leaders should read. Taylor's stories illustrate the power of leading with hospitality and help provide a step by step guide to tap into the heart and minds of those one leads. The stories and experiences Taylor shares are authentic, very relatable, and easy to understand so they can be put into practical use for personal growth as well. Hospitality in 2021 and beyond will take touching people's hearts and *Lead with Hospitality* captures this beautifully."

—Lindell Skinner, senior manager of food and beverage at Disneyland Resort

"*Lead with Hospitality* is the well timed leadership success manual for 2021 and beyond. It outlines a recipe to tap into the hearts and minds of people in a way that will bring out the best of those we lead. Leaders who follow this recipe will create experiences where both employees and customers will feel and see the difference. I look forward to sharing this book with both my team and podcast listeners."

—Arthur Keith, managing director of The Statler Hotel
at Cornell University and host of the
What Do You Stand For? podcast

"Through entertaining anecdotes, relevant statistics, personal experiences and inspiring quotes, Taylor Scott encapsulates the heart of the hospitality industry and presents it to the reader as a valuable tool for becoming an effective leader in any walk of life. From his first visit to 'Wally World' as a child, to his rich career in hospitality, Taylor shares his valuable experiences with warmth and intellect, and even supplies his readers with action plans at the end of each chapter to implement his lessons in the workplace. Both emerging and experienced leaders will benefit from Leading with Hospitality by learning to Connect, Serve, Engage, and Inspire!"

—Doug Lord, regional vice president (west)
of Great Wolf Lodge

"Emerging leaders are cautioned to lead by example, be authentic, and seek advice from experienced leaders. All good insights, but when and where do you go to fulfill this quest? With a proven passion for hospitality, Taylor Scott, writes for those who want to expand their leadership horizons. His latest book is for the readers who are seeking advice, looking to expand, and who want to see the world in a more positive light. A virtual buffet of great examples, shared experiences, stories of success and failure, Taylor has given his followers a practical guide to growing their own leadership style."

—Larry Ross, PhD, emeritus professor at Barnett School
of Free Enterprise, Florida Southern College

"Leading with hospitality is a much needed topic to explore in today's business landscape and an excellent foundation for any leader. Taylor does an amazing job at illustrating the topic and style through his gift of storytelling and relevant experience, while tying in real-world examples and exercises. I highly recommend this book to tenured and emerging leaders, looking to lead with purpose and hospitality."

—Sonny Ritacca, president of Advanced Sales Consulting

"Taylor captures the spirit of hospitality and purpose of leadership in this wonderful read. The same emotional intention used to craft truly great customer experiences can be used to deliver an equally great employee experience."

—Shane Green, internationally recognized culture coach, author of *Culture Hacker*, and president and founder of SGEi and founder of LXbD

"I had the pleasure of working alongside Taylor and can speak first-hand to his unique ability to connect and lead with heart. *Lead with Hospitality* will equip readers with principles to inspire their teams to bring true hospitality into action."

—Rick Jordan, senior director of talent acquisition at Dick's Sporting Goods

Lead with Hospitality

Lead with Hospitality

Be Human.
Emotionally Connect.
Serve Selflessly.

Taylor Scott

Matt Holt Books
An Imprint of BenBella Books, Inc.
Dallas, TX

BenBella Books, Inc.
10440 N. Central Expressway
Suite 800
Dallas, TX 75231
www.benbellabooks.com
Send feedback to feedback@benbellabooks.com

BenBella is a federally registered trademark.

Printed in the United States of America
10 9 8 7 6 5 4 3 2 1

Library of Congress Control Number: 2020053195
ISBN 9781950665945 (print)
ISBN 9781953295224 (electronic)

Editing by Claire Schulz
Proofreading by Kimberly Broderick
    and Greg Teague
Text design and composition
    by PerfecType, Nashville, TN

Copyediting by Gin Kiser
Cover design by Heather Butterfield
Cover image © the Noun Project
Printed by Lake Book Manufacturing

Distributed to the trade by Two Rivers Distribution, an Ingram brand
www.tworiversdistribution.com

Special discounts for bulk sales are available.
Please contact bulkorders@benbellabooks.com.

For the next generation of leaders,
passionate about *connecting, striving for self-mastery,
serving, engaging, coaching, and inspiring*.

It's your time.

Welcome.

CONTENTS

Foreword by Jon Gordon   xvii

Introduction   1

PART ONE CONNECT
CHAPTER 1: Welcome
Creating a Space Where People Will Stay   17

    Find the Elephant in the Room   18

    Wally World through the Eyes of a Child   19

    You're Welcome Here   22

    When They Feel Welcome   23

    Emotional Connection   24

    Help Them Relax   24

    Put Their Minds at Ease   25

    Establish Credibility   27

    Have Fun   29

    Put *Hospitality in Action*—Activating a Sense of Welcome   29

CHAPTER 2: Acceptance
Accepting Yourself, Accepting Others, and Accepting
Organizational Realities   31

  The Accepting Leader   32

  Everyone *Feels* Accepted at Kimpton   34

  How Times Have Changed   36

  Accept Organizational Realities   38

  Put *Hospitality in Action*—Activating Acceptance   43

Action Plan to Lead with Hospitality: CONNECT   44

PART TWO SERVE

CHAPTER 3: Empathy
Understanding Before Explanation Wins Over Hearts and Minds   51

  Leadership Empathy   54

  A Tale of Two Leaders: The Superhuman Leader
    versus the Human Leader   55

  Seek Understanding   57

  Vocalize Your Understanding   59

  Be Willing to Adapt   60

  Put *Hospitality in Action*—Activating Empathy   62

CHAPTER 4: Service
To Serve Is to LEAD—Listen, Educate, Act, Deliver   63

  The Impact of Serving Your Team   69

  How to Serve with LEAD   70

  When You Serve Others, They Pay It Forward   76

Get in the Sauce 79

Put *Hospitality in Action*—Activating Service 80

Action Plan to Lead with Hospitality: SERVE 82

PART THREE ENGAGE

CHAPTER 5: Comfort

*Curiosity, Conversations, and Relationships Happen
Where People Feel Secure* 89

Make Them Feel Comfortable 91

Conversations and Collaboration 92

Curiosity 94

Relationships 95

Belonging 97

Put *Hospitality in Action*—Activating Comfort 98

CHAPTER 6: Genuine Kindness

A Gift Worth Giving because It's Always Well Received 101

Kindness Is Truly a Gift 102

GiVE 103

Kindness Is Contagious 105

Kindness Is Inspiring 106

Put *Hospitality in Action*—Activating Kindness 108

CHAPTER 7: Encouragement

*Uplifting People Fuels Hearts, Which Fuels Minds,
Which Fuels Successful Teams* 109

Recognition: Sawubona Means "We See You" 111

In Transition   112

At Least They See Me   113

Reminders   115

Assistance: Be Like Joe   118

Put *Hospitality in Action*—Activating Encouragement   122

Action Plan to Lead with Hospitality: ENGAGE   125

PART FOUR INSPIRE

CHAPTER 8: Importance

Once People Feel Significant, They Lean In, Step Up,
and Deliver Their Best   131

Make Them Feel Important   133

The Story of Sally and Significance   135

Purpose   138

A True "Importance" Story   142

Fulfillment   145

Put *Hospitality in Action*—Activating Importance   149

CHAPTER 9: Grace

Amazing Grace Wins Every Time   151

Graceful Actions   153

Generous Explanations   154

Forgiveness   156

Last Chance U   159

Your Own Leadership Docuseries   163

Put *Hospitality in Action*—Activating Grace   164

CHAPTER 10: Planning and Coaching
*Strategic Planning Charts the Course, and Effective
Coaching Steers the Ship*   167

  Simple Planning Goes a Long Way   168
  Your Personal Disney Vacation Club Guide   168
  Sales Is Leadership, and Leadership Is Sales   173
  Help Them Set SMART Goals   174
  How Are You Spending Your Time?   176
  Let It Go   179
  Tough Accountability Conversations   180
  Put *Hospitality in Action*—Activating Strategic
     Planning and Coaching   183

CHAPTER 11: Inspiration
*Why People Do More, Become Their Best, and Deliver
Their Best Work*   185

  What Scholars Found about Inspiration   186
  Storytime   190
  Stories to Tell   192
  Experiences   194
  Creating Self-Motivating Environments   196
  Meaningful Work   198
  Put *Hospitality in Action*—Activating Inspiration   199

Action Plan to Lead with Hospitality: INSPIRE   202

Conclusion   207
Acknowledgments   213

Appendix: My Hospitality Journey   217

Connect with Taylor   225

Notes   229

About the Author   233

FOREWORD

You've likely experienced amazing hospitality from a restaurant, bar, hotel, resort, theme park, airline, or casino. The experience left you emotionally connected to the brand, the people who served you, or perhaps even connected to the people who joined you for the meal, hotel stay, flight, craft cocktail, beer, or simply a glass of wine.

Those feelings inspired you to tell stories and reminisce about it. And you were compelled to visit again and again, engaging on a deeper, more personal level with each additional experience. The *feelings* and *emotions* the experience sparked on the inside compelled and inspired you into action on the outside.

It's also likely that at this point in your life and career, you've experienced inspirational leaders who've helped, taught, encouraged, coached, and inspired you to get outside your comfort zone, or motivated you to become the best version of yourself.

What was it about their leadership styles, their character as human beings, or the environment they created that inspired you to do more for your team and ultimately for your own growth, personally or professionally? I'd be willing to bet it was *how those leaders made you feel.*

Taylor Scott has written a book creatively linking the essence of gracious hospitality to the foundations of inspiring, transformational leadership. As you read each chapter, you'll *experience* Taylor's own brand of leadership and hospitality as he unpacks proven leadership principles, inspirational stories, and actionable applications for how you can transform jobs into meaningful work for those you lead, and inspire them to do their best work.

What's special about this book is that Taylor's style of writing aligns with how he recommends leading, which is to *connect, serve, engage,* and *inspire,* in that order. You'll feel *a personal connection* with his relatable authenticity. You'll be *well served* with the leadership and life lessons he shares. You'll be *engaged* as he encourages you. And you'll certainly be *inspired* by his gift of storytelling.

Before my career as an author and speaker, I owned and operated restaurants myself. I understand the mental, physical, and emotional demands of the hospitality industry as well as the brand of leadership it takes to continually connect with and inspire teams to achieve and deliver desired results. That's why I have so much respect and admiration for Taylor's dynamic ability to lead teams in various lines of business for world-class hospitality and entertainment organizations such as the Walt Disney Company, Gaylord Hotels and Resorts, Wynn Resorts, and The Cosmopolitan of Las Vegas.

When Taylor reached out to connect with me, I sensed his passion, purpose, and sense of urgency to get this book into the world so that he could *connect with* and *inspire* as many people as he could at a time when people need inspiration the most.

My life's work and underlying purpose is to write books, create learning experiences, and deliver inspirational keynotes on the power of positive leadership. Positive leaders can change the game for any team, organization, or company because they drive *positive cultures*.

Follow Taylor's positivity, advice, and recommendations for how to lead with hospitality in your heart, and you'll be not only in the driver's seat of the energy bus in your organization but also in your own life.

Thank you, Taylor, for showing us how leading with hospitality helps us make a positive impact, have fun, and enjoy the ride.

—Jon Gordon

Bestselling author of *The Energy Bus*,

The Carpenter, and *The Power of Positive Leadership*

INTRODUCTION

S
ummer Grace graduated from college a few years ago, excited to begin her career. She was thrilled to find a job with a reputable brand in an industry she had been interested in since high school. Since she started, her career has been an up-and-down adventure.

During the interview process, it felt like she and her future boss, Derek, had known each other for years. Through two phone conversations and one in-person meeting, Derek expressed what felt like a genuine interest in Summer as a person, not just as a potential employee. He wanted to understand everything he could about how and where she grew up, her favorite sports, and most importantly, her future dreams and aspirations. The two immediately connected.

Summer answered his questions, sharing bits and pieces about who she was and what she wanted to do. Derek listened attentively and then shared more about his career and vision for the future of his organization. Her enthusiasm grew as she envisioned a future with him as a leader. Accepting the job offer was simple and stress-free.

In the middle of her commute to work one day a year later, she reflected on her experiences up to that point. In her first few weeks, she had connected with Derek and her coworkers. She quickly and easily made new friends, especially with one colleague, Amanda. Training was fun, insightful, and made her more excited about her newfound company, colleagues, and community. She was a nervous wreck at first, but those nerves quickly gave way to confidence. When Derek and others touched base to make sure she had everything she needed, she felt important. She was certain she belonged exactly where she had landed.

Over the months, Summer's confidence in her ability to perform, succeed, and grow had soared. The more time she spent with her new friends in the office, the more connected she felt. Most nights on her way home, she'd call her mom with updates on the exciting projects she was assigned and inspiring conversations she enjoyed with Derek and her coworkers. She was full of passion and purpose.

Summer's team, her peers, and even partners in other departments loved her. Everyone called Summer when they felt down. She encouraged them and lifted them up. She came in early, stayed late, and remained available on weekends, ready to lend an ear to those who needed it.

But, slowly, she noticed a shift in her boss. Derek was less available. Even though she worked harder and delivered better results than anyone in her group, it never seemed good enough. The harder she worked, the more Derek questioned everything, from her approach to her performance. The communication and connection she had experienced those early months gave way to sparse, sporadic conversations, and no more one-on-ones with Derek. His negativity and lack of interest made her feel uncomfortable and judged every morning as she walked through the doors.

It seemed like she wasn't the only one. Her coworkers gradually became nervous and worried about the future. Some of her colleagues started finding other jobs.

She became aware with blinding clarity why coworkers had turned to her when they felt down. Summer was more of a supportive leader than Derek, so they reached out to her for encouragement more than they reached out to him.

Summer's industriousness gave way to complacency. Her sense of purpose and determination to give her best all but disappeared. The enthusiasm that had fueled her before was replaced with bitterness. She usually was the positive one, the encourager. She no longer possessed the emotional energy to be the cheerleader, advocate, or uplifting teammate she once had been. Gradually, the only reason her leaders called were during those infrequent moments when they told her what was wrong with her work and what assignments were late.

Perhaps more disappointing, Summer's confidence was shaken. She always counted on it to propel her through any doubts or fears. Two weeks ago, she had felt defeated. Summer had gone home and applied for twelve jobs online. She had gone to four interviews and received a job offer. Wondering why she'd lost her energy and enthusiasm, Summer was torn between taking a new job she wasn't sure about, or staying in the job she once loved but had grown to hate.

Just then, Summer's phone buzzed with an incoming call from her friend and former coworker Amanda. She exited the freeway and pulled into a parking lot to answer. The two had become close during training and remained friends since Amanda had left the company six months prior. The job offer was why she wanted to talk to Amanda. She needed advice. Summer needed to talk to someone who understood.

Amanda was happy to carve out time.

Summer explained to Amanda how things had gone south over the last year.

Amanda knew what was coming, but she let Summer get it off her chest. She always listened empathetically, which is why Summer's relationship with Amanda developed so quickly and remained intact despite Amanda's departure from the company.

Amanda asked, "Why did you start looking for new jobs?"

Her left hand rested on her forehead as she captured the tears escaping from the corners of her eyes. Summer said, "I don't like how Derek makes me feel."

With an empathetic tone, Amanda said, "I didn't either. That's why I left."

Summer accepted the new job offer the next day. She started over with a new company, new coworkers, and a new leader she hoped would encourage her, guide her and make her *feel* better about herself, her role, and her opportunity for professional and personal growth.

Leaders of the Next Generation, We Have an Opportunity

If you relate to the parable of Summer, Amanda, and Derek, you're not alone.

O. C. Tanner Institute's 2020 Culture Report says, "If offered a job at a different company with a similar role, pay, and benefits, a little over half (59 percent) of employees would accept the job."[1] So as you read this (at least at the time of this writing), over half the workforce is looking for greener pastures.

There's more.

Millennials, who comprise over half of the American workforce, say they're hungry to learn so they can become better, more impactful leaders. They, along with Generation Z, now starting to enter the workforce, aren't receiving the education, mentorship, and inspiration they deserve to achieve the career fulfillment they desperately desire. Not surprisingly, the Gallup organization reveals that an overwhelming majority of employees are disengaged.[2]

According to Work Institute's 2019 Retention Report, turnover is anticipated to hit record highs, costing US companies over $600 *billion*. One in three workers is projected to *voluntarily* leave their job each year by 2023.[3] People are willing start over, leaving their former company on the never-ending treadmill of *replacing, restructuring,* and *rebuilding* their teams and organizational cultures.

Analysts estimate employee turnover costs approximately $15,000 per worker. Half of employees who voluntarily left a job in 2018 went looking for greener pastures due to a lack of career development, no work/life balance, or as a result of a manager's behavior. All things that good leadership has the potential to change.

Fellow leaders and future executives, business owners, and entrepreneurs, we have an opportunity here. We know we can do better. We can and we will do better.

With the right mindset, frontline and middle managers can create productive, meaningful environments where employees feel safe and become their best selves, delivering their best work.

You probably know people like Summer and Amanda. They may be on your team. Or their story may be the same as yours. You expect more from your leaders and want to be better for those you lead. When people in leadership roles fail to actually lead, encourage, or make sure their teams feel valued, the most valuable people leave first. The company lost a top-notch producer willing to go the extra mile with tremendous leadership potential when Summer handed Derek her resignation.

My hope for you and for your organization is that everyone from your top performers to your up-and-comers begin to feel differently about you as their leader and, in turn, more encouraged and inspired than ever to deliver their best work for your organization.

Why We Need to Lead with Hospitality

Do you have a favorite hotel? What about a favorite restaurant, lounge, or bar? Is there a vacation destination that always makes you feel comfortable; almost as if you were at home? A favorite cruise line or ship? How about airlines?

Now that your mind is in vacation mode or enjoying thoughts about where you used to go with the family, is that one special hospitality experience, person, or place dancing in your head?

Why do we have favorite hotels, restaurants, bars, resorts, and even a favorite airline? Is it *what* we can do while there? Is it *why* we return again and again? Maybe it's a little of both. Now think about the *how*. How do those hotels, restaurants, lounges, bars, or airlines make you feel?

The properties are amazing, and the products are top notch. They have a reputation for creating memorable experiences. However, they're truly remarkable because of *how they made us feel back then and how they still make us feel today.* Those are feelings worth returning to over and over and experiences that give us great stories to share. Beyond the stories are the specific actions we're inspired to take.

Before you know it, you're spending more money at the lobby bar and booking another dinner reservation. You're applying for the credit card aligned with the airline you love, so you can earn enough points to be a passenger on another flight.

And in all my travels and experiences, working with and for some of the most game-changing brands in the world, I've realized an interesting truth.

We love our favorite hotels, restaurants, lounges, bars, and airlines for the same reasons we love our favorite leaders and companies where we work or worked in the past. We love them because we feel connected to them, and that connection is almost always a function of *how they make us feel*.

That truth applies to the people on your team. So many people long for that feeling in their own lives and careers, to be led with genuine hospitality. This book is about the *feelings* that move people to move in purposeful and productive ways—including inspired action, peak performance, and of course, delivering results, all while making both money and meaning at the same time. My goal is to illustrate the connecting thread between genuine *hospitality* and inspiring *leadership*.

Lead with Hospitality is for leaders who strive to create relationships, a culture of belonging, and meaningful work for those they lead. It's also for leaders who have accepted the challenge and responsibility of leadership because they care about people and they're compelled to inspire, motivate, and transform groups of people into high-performing teams of people.

If that describes you, welcome aboard.

Why Should You Believe Me?

I love all facets of hospitality and leadership. Both inspire me to care more, love more, serve more, and do more for people. The only thing I love more than becoming inspired myself is inspiring others.

That's why I wrote this book.

In 2003, the executive vice president of operations at Walt Disney World Resort was Lee Cockerell. He gave me some advice that I've taken seriously since the day we met all those years ago.

He said, "Spend the first ten to fifteen years of your career gaining as much experience in as many different lines of business as possible. Discover your true passion and then do that the rest of your life."

Teaching, coaching, writing, and speaking are my true passions. However, I write books, inspire people, connect with audiences, and train up-and-coming leaders as a result of everything I've learned working, living, learning, and leading in the hospitality industry since 1998.

My twenty-year journey in thirty seconds sounds like this:

- Walt Disney World Resort
- Gaylord Palms Resort and Convention Center—Opening Team
- Disney's Pop Century Resort—Opening Team
- Disney Destinations, LLC
- Encore at Wynn Las Vegas—Encore Opening Team
- The Cosmopolitan of Las Vegas—Opening Team
- Disney Vacation Club at the Disneyland Resort

> Throughout my professional career I've been blessed with opportunity after opportunity to work for and represent some of the most highly sought-after, game-changing brands in the world. I didn't always realize it at the time, but each career stop has in some way, shape, or form *positively changed the game* for people inside and outside their organizations. For more on this, please see the appendix.

Along the way, I attended graduate school at Cornell University's School of Hotel Administration. And today, as an author, speaker, and leadership-development consultant, I'm hired to teach, coach, and inspire teams and leaders across the country on the topics of leadership, teamwork, and personal growth.

As mentioned, I love it all: from hotels to bars to restaurants to airlines to rental car, and yes, even retail, with those crazy hours. I've flipped burgers, worked a fryer full of chicken fingers, stocked shelves, worked cash registers, operated theme park attractions, checked people in and out of hotels, made beds, cleaned toilets, folded laundry, parked cars, delivered luggage, served food, and served people.

I've led teams in housekeeping, bell services, front desk, travel-industry sales, casino marketing, vacation-ownership sales, and private-club sales. I've opened four mega-resort hotels on grand-opening teams, launched brands, and developed online marketing platforms. This journey has taken me from a small town in eastern Kentucky where I grew up, to *experiencing* life in central Florida, south Florida, upstate New York, Las Vegas, and Southern California.

I consider myself blessed beyond my wildest dreams because, before I lived or worked anywhere, I first dreamed of living and working in all these places. The journey hasn't always been filled with rainbows, pixie dust, butterflies, and cocktails with a view. It hasn't been without failure, worry, doubt, or fear. I've simply experienced enough, good and bad, to share with you what works and what doesn't work, as it pertains to *becoming a successful leader, inspiring people, and enjoying your own life.*

Who This Book Is For

Early in my journey I had lofty but, in my mind, achievable career goals. I wanted to become a leader of people, creating positive, innovative change in exciting places for great companies.

Perhaps you share similar career and life goals.

I remember wondering how in the world I'd ever *get noticed* and then *get selected* so I could give all I could to positively change the game for people and the companies where I worked. I read many great books that inspired me, challenged me, and taught me.

This book is for you if you're new to leadership in any industry. If you recently received a promotion or the opportunity and responsibility to lead people but you don't know where to start, this book will help. It was also written for senior leaders of organizations who value these traits, and would like to inspire, educate, and coach leaders in their organizations to lead with hospitality, putting into practice the thoughts, ideals, and tactics you're about to read and *experience*.

This book is for you, to lift you up, inspire you, challenge you, and teach you how to **get noticed, get selected,** and **give your heart** so you completely **change the game** for your team and yourself.

Here's a Preview of What You're about to Read

This book is divided into four parts:

Part One: Connect
Part Two: Serve
Part Three: Engage
Part Four: Inspire

If any one of these steps is taken out of order, it compromises a leader's ability to appeal to the specific *emotions* that give people the energy and enthusiasm to *move, take action, change behavior, become their best,* or *deliver their best work.* When leaders first connect on a human level, teams open up and feel welcome, comfortable, and important enough to take risks and do their best work.

For example, if you try to coach and inspire before you've earned enough respect and credibility to do so, your message will fall flat, and people will distance themselves from you. Spending time and energy connecting with people on a personal level and attending to their needs first before asking anything of them earns you two things: respect and credibility. We'll unpack how selflessly serving others by giving them your time, talent, and heart will pave the way for you to lead yourself and others to success and happiness at work and at home.

Throughout these pages I'll share stories, illustrations, and applications to change your relationships at work and home, which will, in turn, change your life. In each chapter, you'll read stories from my own journey as well as stories of great leaders from a variety of professions who show how the principles of gracious hospitality can be put to work. Each of the book's four parts ends with specific prompts and exercises you can use to put these ideas into action right away. The coolest part is it'll also change the lives of those you lead, which is why we all accept the responsibility of leadership.

My hope is this book will provide you with an inspirational and efficient roadmap for leading your teams and yourself to success.

Leadership Can Be Different and a More Meaningful Experience for Everyone

For the next generation, leadership can be different and better than it's been in recent years. The culture where you work can be better. Turnover rates could be cut in half. Productivity among your team and in your organization can rise. The people you lead will do more, become more, and deliver much more with your leadership.

O. C. Tanner Institute's research reveals progress was made between their 2018 Culture Report and the most recent 2020 Culture Report. While we're moving in the right direction, we still have work to do in the 2020s and beyond.[4]

Here's what their research tells us about the slight progress from 2018 to 2020 in *how* employees felt about their workplace culture:

- 71 percent of people feel a sense of purpose, up from 66 percent in 2018
- 66 percent of people feel a sense of opportunity, up from 59 percent in 2018
- 67 percent of people feel a sense of success, up from 60 percent in 2018
- 62 percent of people feel a sense of appreciation, up from 57 percent in 2018
- 54 percent of people feel a sense of well-being, up from 53 percent in 2018
- 61 percent of people feel a sense of leadership, up from 57 percent in 2018

While the progress is encouraging, you can see how many employees are still feeling like Summer and Amanda. Inevitably, many people feel like you may have felt in a past or current role, with an uninspiring leader. Maybe you even feel that way today. Perhaps your employees or those you lead feel this way.

Whether you're helping your organization rebuild or bounce back, or even if you're leading your team through a season of growth or preparing yourself for personal and professional growth of your own, this is your opportunity to meet this moment. With simple changes to your approach, you can change how people feel about work. When you influence and change how people feel, you'll change what people do. Even more impactful than changing *what they do*, you'll change *how they do it*. They'll do more, become more, and deliver more, for you and on your behalf, because of how you make them feel.

I wrote this book to inspire and encourage you to change how your employees and your organization *feel* about work. As you change how they feel, you'll feel better. The better you feel, the better they feel, and the more successful and happier everyone will be.

Bad days can be transformed into better, more inspiring days when you lead with hospitality.

Change Lives and Make a Positive Impact

You could be that leader who changes someone's life, making a positive impact so they become compelled to inspire someone else. That's the magic of leading with hospitality in everything you do.

It's contagious, and it's meaningful. You could be the leader who finally brings your team to the next level of productivity, profitability, or purpose your organization needed from your predecessors but simply hasn't experienced for years.

In the process, you'll be noticed by your leaders, and selected for more projects, promotions, and exposure. As you *give* your heart to others, you'll change the game for yourself and your organization. If you want to

- engage your teams in new, stimulating ways,
- change the culture where you work,
- transform ordinary jobs into meaningful work for your team and yourself, and
- lead and inspire your team to deliver those ever-important results for senior leaders or the board of directors,

then you've picked up the right book.

Maya Angelou was on to something when she famously said, "At the end of the day, people won't remember what you said or did. They will remember how you made them feel."[5] For those of us who lead with hospitality, the quote above is especially resonant.

This book is about how to make your greatest asset in business and life—your people—feel *welcome, comfortable,* and *important.* Magic unfolds when you intentionally lead with hospitality.

So welcome! Thanks for picking up this book. Together, we'll unpack this simple principle of leadership—*before anyone is inspired to do anything, they must first feel something.*

For the next couple hours, the most important person in my life is you. My passion is to encourage people with uplifting stories and experiences. My purpose is to help leaders like you transform ordinary jobs into meaningful work for those you lead. Leading with hospitality inspires new levels of activity, productivity, and profitability for your organization. In this way your teams, your organization, and you will enjoy success and more meaning at work and in your personal life. You opened this book for a reason, and you're the reason I wrote it.

Sit back, relax, and enjoy the ride.

PART ONE

CONNECT

Chapter 1

WELCOME

Creating a Space Where People Will Stay

A great restaurant is one that just makes you feel like you're unsure whether you went out or you came home . . . If it can do both of those things at the same time, you're hooked.

—Danny Meyer

I was in my first full-time leadership role in the hospitality industry, as a housekeeping manager for the grand opening of the beautiful Gaylord Palms Resort and Convention Center in Kissimmee, Florida. I was twenty-two years old, fired up, and full of energy as I gazed out to the classic atrium for which Gaylord Hotels and Resorts are known. That was the backdrop to a guest speaker our general manager had invited to inspire us. I don't recall the speaker's name or much from his speech. However, I remember one timeless, transferable leadership principle that has rung in my head every day since.

He said, "You're working in the dynamic business of hospitality. Whether you work in hospitality for the next couple years or the next twenty years, remember: the essence of true hospitality is the ability to make people feel **welcome, comfortable,** and **important.**"

Nearly two decades later, I'm convinced the essence of dynamic, inspirational *leadership* is also the ability to make *people feel* welcome, comfortable, and important. Welcome is a crucial first step.

Find the Elephant in the Room

Before we get into how to make people feel welcome, you may be wondering why I'm paying so much attention to the importance of feeling. Isn't good leadership all about getting good results?

Well, in his book *The Happiness Hypothesis*, NYU psychologist Jonathan Haidt used an analogy that paints the picture of what's going on inside the human brain at all times.[6] Science tells us that we have two systems in our brains: an emotional side of the brain and a logical side of the brain. Haidt's analogy of the human brain is an elephant with a person riding it, saddled up on its back.

The *rider* illustrates the logical side of the brain, which is responsible for reasoning, analyzing, planning, and our intellectual understanding. The *elephant* illustrates the emotional side of the brain, which is of course responsible for emotions and instinctively *feeling* pain or pleasure.

Consider the metaphor of a human rider perched atop a six-ton elephant. While the rider may provide the analytical support to move or go in a certain direction (*or change behavior*), the elephant, with a six-ton weight advantage, however, provides the energy to move. If the rider and the elephant ever disagree, the elephant will always overpower the rider. This is why change is so hard and why it can be difficult to lead certain people to do certain things. If they don't *feel* it, they won't *do* it.

To inspire and motivate people, sure, we have to "direct the rider," giving clear expectations and the information, tools, and support for them to succeed. More importantly, as Jonathan Haidt's analogy depicts, to inspire action, leaders have to find and motivate "the elephant." That is to say, leaders have to appeal to the emotions of those they lead.

Leading with hospitality is an approach, mentality, and a lifestyle that mixes the art of leadership with the science of behavioral psychology described above. Great leaders understand that before anyone is compelled to *do* anything, they must first *feel*. Leading with hospitality guides you in how to find and motivate "the elephants" in the room. Follow these steps and you'll connect with people on a human level, which allows you to take them to the next level when it comes to your team's relationships with each other and the results they'll consistently deliver.

Wally World Through the Eyes of a Child

Think back to that special vacation with your family or loved ones back when you stayed in a nice hotel. Regardless of your destination, if it rushes to your mind right now, then by default it must have been memorable. It likely started with a welcome or an arrival experience you remember to this day.

I have had many memorable hotel and restaurant experiences throughout my life, but one early experience particularly sticks in my mind. When I was five years old, my parents took my sister and me to Orlando. It was our first trip to Walt Disney World Resort, and we stayed at the Royal Plaza on Hotel Plaza Boulevard (now operating as the B Resort & Spa). It's on Disney property, but it's not an official owned-and-operated Disney Resort.

The anticipation had been building for weeks. Expectations for our trip, the rides, fun, swimming, and pure vacationing were at an all-time high for my five-year-old brain and my sister's three-year-old heart and soul. Visions of princesses probably danced in her head.

Imagine my parents: a couple twenty-somethings from Kentucky, loading their two young children in a minivan, stocking coolers and suitcases, and putting what would become dreams and memories on their credit cards that they'd spend a year paying off, just to take us on vacation. (We didn't know it at the time, but actually, this trip would become an annual tradition for our family throughout my childhood and teenage years. Thanks, Mom and Dad, for taking us on vacation and introducing me to the magic of hospitality.)

With my sister and me loudly unleashing our excitement from the backseat of the minivan and my parents' nervous thoughts of *I hope this works out*, the Scotts arrived for a week of family fun in 1985. The Royal Plaza was great hotel, with all the usual amenities: an expansive pool, a solid restaurant, comfortable bar, and old-school, large rooms. Because it was on Walt Disney World property, we could see the fireworks from our room on an upper floor.

I remember bits and pieces of the trip, but I recall little of the attractions, dinners, lunches, character breakfasts, and the experiences for which my parents spent an arm and a leg. (I mean, in my defense, I was five years old.)

I *do* remember the moment we pulled into the front drive. The doorman that evening made us feel incredibly welcome. My sister and I jumped out of the car, probably looking like Kevin McAllister in *Home Alone*. (Remember the scene when he runs through the house as he realizes his family left him alone for the holidays, jumping on beds, running up and down stairs, and screaming at the top of his lungs?)

The doorman looked at our family as my mom corralled my sister and me and said, "Welcome to the Royal Plaza! Are y'all going to Wally World?"

Speaking of John Hughes movies, the original version of *National Lampoon's Vacation*, with Chevy Chase as Clark Griswold driving his family to Wally World, was released in 1983. This was just over a year later. Of course, my family thought the movie was hilarious. I hadn't seen the movie at the tender age of five, but I heard my parents talk about it. We talked about it, quoted lines from it, and laughed about the Griswolds' misadventures. (Actually, we *still* quote silly lines and laugh about that movie. And we still refer to Walt Disney World as "Wally World." Who doesn't?)

So I knew enough to know this doorman, working the late shift in Orlando on an eighty-five-degree night on the front drive of the Royal Plaza, made my parents crack up laughing. That was cool, for a young boy to see his parents *feel* so joyful at the most magical place on Earth.

He followed up his opening "Wally World" comment with welcoming words, directions, and an orientation to the property. He told us where the amenities were: the front desk, pool, bus stop, laundry room, and the restaurant where we could have breakfast before going to the park.

My parents instantly felt welcome. My sister and I felt welcome because my parents felt welcome. That small yet powerful interaction with our hotel doorman started our vacation off on the right, light-hearted foot. Laughter replaced my parents' nervous, worried energy. That welcome feeling laid the foundation for a great vacation. The anxiety-ridden expectations they felt were suddenly replaced with joy and relaxation.

You're Welcome Here

Can we all agree people stay where they feel welcome? They stay and enjoy places and the people who help them feel a tremendous sense of ease and being embraced. This is the first transferable truth of the spirit and essence of *hospitality*, in the context of leadership.

If you grab a dictionary and look up the word *hospitality*, you'll see that it's defined as "the friendly and generous reception and entertainment of guests, visitors, or strangers."

As leaders, we have many deliverables, to-dos, and responsibilities on our plate. We're expected to drive results on numerous fronts: financial, culture changing, team building, process improvement, customer service scores, and whatever else comes up in board meetings or the C suite. Yet rising to the role of manager, director, or vice president is only half the battle. Once you're there, inspiring appropriate action and productivity are among the first of many tall tasks that await leaders.

This may sound glaringly obvious, but it's worth stating to introduce the importance of *leading with hospitality*. The extent to which any leader is successful in leading a team depends to a large degree on whether team members are compelled to follow them, as their leader. The first step in getting anyone to follow you as a respected leader is to first and foremost **make them feel welcome.**

If they feel welcome, they'll stay on your team, in your corner, on your side, and with your organization. (Remember: as I mentioned in the introduction, one in three workers were expected to voluntarily leave their jobs in the coming years.[7]) Perhaps more important than people staying with your organization is the work they do and how they perform while a part of it.

They'll begin to enjoy your presence and delivering results for you and on your behalf.

When They Feel Welcome

Here's what happens when people genuinely feel welcome. They begin to feel the following:

- Relaxed and safe, which allows them to be themselves. (That's why you hired them. So, you'll want them to be *"them"* as much as possible. We'll return to this idea in chapter 2.)
- Open-minded, which sparks their creativity for new, fresh ideas. (We'll return to this idea in chapter 5.)
- Less anxious and fearful, and more energetic, enthusiastic, and committed.
- They begin to truly enjoy their experience, which makes them more loyal.

It's Not Just About Happy Employees

When your employees feel welcome, they will enjoy their experience working on your team and in your presence. But if that's not enough incentive for you, know that your guests, customers, and clients will most certainly see and feel it too.

When your guests, customers, and clients see and feel it, you're well on your way to developing a sustainable, profitable business. Why? Because they'll return again and again, while telling stories about their experience to anyone who'll listen on Facebook, Twitter, Instagram, and Snapchat, not to mention at the grocery store, coffee shop, or gym or on a plane.

If you inspire joy among your team members, which, by the way, consistently delivers results, you'll absolutely get noticed by your own leaders as well as by your peers.

This domino effect of positive results will start simply because you first made members of your team feel *welcome*.

Emotional Connection

Just like with our favorite hotels, restaurants, cruise lines, lounges, or any brand, once we feel more welcome, we naturally connect emotionally. Those emotional connections are like steroids to any relationship. In fact, the emotional connection to any person, place, or brand not only draws us in, but also compels us to tell stories about them, which evokes a feeling we want to return to, day after day. In other words, the emotion or feeling drives decisions to act or change behavior. Since leadership is about inspiring, motivating, and *leading* others toward a goal, cause, or mission, evoking this emotional connection is fundamental to any leader's success.

So how can you go about welcoming your team to foster this emotional connection? There are four things a great leader should do to make sure their teams feel welcome:

1. Help them relax.
2. Put their minds at ease.
3. Establish credibility.
4. Have fun!

Help Them Relax

We've all been there. It's the first day, first week, first meeting, or any of all the other firsts of a new job. It's a time that's anything but relaxing for most people. While some leaders, whether they're managers, directors, or vice presidents, will take this opportunity to set the tone to prove their power and awesomeness, other more hospitable leaders will do the opposite and leverage the opportunity right out the gate to help their new team or team member relax and feel welcome.

Leading with genuine hospitality, helping them relax, is a powerful way to impact change while getting the most out of each person. They have the talent, but deploying and channeling their talent, purposefully and intentionally, to drive results is up to you as their leader. So make them feel welcome, and you'll be on your way to do just that.

It can be as simple as any of the following gestures:

+ Let them know how grateful you are to have them on your team.
+ Introduce them to as many people as possible, as a connector and facilitator of new, budding relationships.
+ Show them around the office, property, neighborhood, or wherever makes sense. (It seems very basic, but start by showing them where the bathrooms are and where they can get food.)

Actually, those top two tips are important whether someone is new to your team or they have been with you for years.

Put Their Minds at Ease

A constant undertone of tension-riddled, lofty expectations hovers over every team in any organization. Managers hire great people for their exceptional talent, charisma, and work ethic. But one thing is certain with every person you hire: they're human like you. So their thoughts and fears may get in their way, especially at first or in the early stages of your relationship.

Leading with hospitality is about being a leader and a champion for your people. It means making sure they understand, no matter what, you're a team. You're there to help them with what they need to succeed. This breaks down the *relationship tension* often present between leader and employee.

- **Let them know you're there to help, not hurt.** Leadership is dynamic. At times, you'll need to coach. At other times, you'll need to hold people accountable. Sometimes, you'll praise, and at other times, you'll certainly offer feedback. Your team needs to know all the above come from a good place, a safe place. Be the leader who puts their mind at ease with a simple message: *you're always there to help, not hurt.*

- **Tell them in their first thirty days to relax, listen, and learn from others.** I once had a boss who, in the middle of my onboarding in a brand-new job, told me, "Don't worry. We're not going to ask you to change the world right away. Relax and get settled in your new surroundings. Get to know the players and key stakeholders. We'll help you with everything." That statement calmed my nerves in the moment and throughout my first year on the job. Give your people that feeling, and it will allow them to relax in the same fashion.

- **Make sure they know it's not all on their shoulders.** Remind them of their specific role on the team. They'll feel better knowing everyone else has a role, and they have a specific role. That will remind them they don't have to do everything alone.

- **Set clear expectations for their performance.** Let them know what you want to see in terms of their performance, contributions, relationships with others, and even their level of enjoyment and fulfillment. When they know you want the best for them personally and professionally, their sense of welcome will skyrocket, and their worries will plummet. That will bode well for their performance.

* **Tell them what *they* can expect if they do well.** For example, let them know just what's in it for them when they execute well. That will do two things: it will absolutely eliminate their worry, and it will give them a sense of purpose. Purpose is like fuel for people's souls, igniting the passion that sparks intentional action, which produces desired results despite inevitable adversities we encounter along the way. (We'll talk more about purpose later.)

People are people. So, chances are, whether they've been there for ninety minutes, ninety days, or nine years, they may have worries swirling in their mind. They might feel concerned about lots of things, including their team, their security in their role, the future of the company, or even the stock market and its impact on your organization. We'll touch on the power of engagement throughout the rest of this book, but perhaps the most important time to engage with employees is within their first few weeks and months on the job.

> According to a survey by Gallup, employees who are engaged are 27 percent more likely to report "excellent" performance.[8]

Establish Credibility

Early on in your relationship with a new team member, it is important to establish credibility, both for the organization and for yourself as a leader. This is a fine line, because while establishing credibility is important, going too far can make you come across as cocky. Instead, be humble and reassure them they made the right decision; they're in a safe place with you. Give them your reasons why that's true. Without bragging, give them the answers to questions like the following:

- How many years have you been in the industry?
- How many years have you been with your company?
- Why do you like working here?
- What is your company's mission? What's your brand all about?
- Has your organization won any awards or been recognized for excellence in some way?

Even if it is simply your enthusiasm, share it. Knowing about your experience or credentials will further calm their nerves and give them a reason to stay with the company for the long haul. One way to establish credibility is to simply communicate the vision and mission of the organization they're now part of creating and delivering. It sounds simple enough, but you'd be surprised how many leaders, whether they're managers, directors, or even vice presidents, who fail to communicate the vision of where they're taking the team.

You can be different. If you're not sure of the overarching vision and mission of your organization as a whole, simply ask your own leaders or peers. More than likely, they'll be able to tell you, and you can do your part as a leader in the organization by sharing the vision with your team. When it comes to your own vision for your team, division, or department, as long as it aligns with where your organization is headed, you get to craft it. When your team knows you have a vision for the team, and especially when they know you envision them as an integral part of the plan to create your vision, you'll gain credibility, and they'll feel welcome on your team.

Have Fun

Be serious about your team, your organization's goals, developing people, and delivering results. However, don't take yourself too seriously. It's a cliché, but it's true. We spend over a third of our lives working, and from time to time, we spend nearly half of our waking hours either at work, talking about work, or working remotely. You might as well enjoy it. If you don't enjoy it, you'll become miserable, your team will be miserable, and your guests, customers, and clients will be miserable too. Even worse, your friends, families, and loved ones will be miserable because they know you're feeling miserable. Fun crushes misery. So lead with hospitality, and crush it when it comes to having fun at work.

 Put *Hospitality in Action*— Activating a Sense of Welcome

1. **Reduce tension early.** Socially engage and personally connect with people on your teams. Connect them to each other as well as your brand. Take time to set up **one-on-one meetings** with each person. At least once a week, schedule **team meetings** that you intentionally prepare with a clearly defined *purpose*, *process*, and *potential payoff*. This will help your team members relax. When they relax, you'll start getting their best performance. That's your job.

2. **Eliminate their worries by setting clear expectations** with honesty and transparency. The more you set the record straight, the fewer doubts, worries, and concerns they'll have, leaving more time and energy for your team to deliver at peak levels.

3. **Acknowledge people, early and often.** Catch them "doing it right," and tell the rest of the team what a great job they did. Tell upper management when you get a chance and let them know you went to bat for them. Blog about it, or even share a story about it on social media. We'll discuss this much more in chapter 7.

4. **Be serious about developing your team, but don't take yourself too seriously.** Never take your eye off the ball regarding your team's ability to execute. But don't take yourself too seriously either. Remember: fun crushes misery, so crush it for your team when it comes to having fun.

5. **Encourage team outings for bonding.** These activities foster blossoming relationships over time. Be that connector and facilitator getting to know people on a human level. Emotional connections will spark around you, which makes for a great culture. Inevitably, great results will follow.

Chapter 2

ACCEPTANCE

*Accepting Yourself, Accepting Others,
and Accepting Organizational Realities*

*We can always choose to perceive things differently. You can focus
on what's wrong in your life, or you can focus on what's right.*
                                              —Marianne Williamson

Have you ever been to a nice hotel or restaurant and felt maybe you arrived a bit underdressed? Or perhaps you were in a hotel lobby or restaurant bar with a group of friends or family and noticed your group was being a bit loud or rambunctious? Whether we're underdressed, too loud, or anything less than ideal, we're still guests in the hotels, restaurants, and bars we visit. They serve us anyway. They don't ask for credentials, your bank statement, a resume, cover letter, or a list of accomplishments. Nope, they smile at you, welcome you into their world, accepting that you're not perfect, just like every other guest. Then they serve you anyway.

Leaders, we are all human—and that means accepting team members for who they are.

The Accepting Leader

As a leader, a big part of making your teams feel welcome is to accept people for who they are as opposed to what they've accomplished. It's all about leading with hospitality, in everything you do. So, like those friendly people at the hotel front desk, along with your favorite bartenders and flight attendants who accept their guests and welcome them in regardless of how they measure up on the surface, leaders win over their teams when they do the same.

Our society isn't really set up like this, so it takes intentional thought, discipline, and work. When you go against the grain with this principle, it has an impact and will make a positive impact on those you lead and people in your life.

For instance, consider what you say when you meet people for the first time. Maybe you chat up another couple on vacation, or you strike up a conversation with the person sitting next to you on the plane. A few minutes into the conversation, someone usually asks, "So, what do you do?" They don't always mean anything by it. It's how our society thinks and behaves. We're generally fixated on work, accomplishments, and status.

If you've ever worked in sales or known anyone in sales, you know it's an accomplishment-driven culture. It's relentless, because in these jobs, you're only as good as your last good day, week, month, or quarter. The demands and pressures to "make your numbers" never go away. At least, that's how it feels. It becomes a slippery slope for sales leaders and salespeople. Leaders tend to push hard, and salespeople begin to believe their value in the world is defined by the numbers they achieve.

And yet, doesn't this also seem to be true beyond the world of sales? The pressure is almost omnipresent across every industry and walk of life. We feel the strain to first accomplish or achieve something. Whether it's a job thing, a life thing, or a relationship thing, we're pressured to achieve, accomplish, or prove our worth so that we can then feel accepted. We want to feel accepted by our bosses, our peers, our families—even the person sitting next to us on the airplane. We need to feel accepted so we can feel significant. That feeling of significance is almost the gateway to feeling confident enough to perform, contribute, or produce. I'll share more about significance later in chapter 8.

Leading with hospitality turns this conventional wisdom on its head. Here's the difference: those who lead with hospitality understand the impact of accepting every person on their team for who they are, right off the bat. To make people feel tremendously connected is to accept them just as they are, understanding that nobody's perfect. However, everyone's capable of performing at their best. It's our job as leaders leading with hospitality to connect with people on a human level so that we can inspire them to go to the next level.

The problem with accepting people only when they achieve certain milestones is that if they fall short, they never feel significant. If they never feel significant, they'll rarely perform to their full potential. If they don't perform, then accomplishments are few and far between for everyone, including the leader.

Something magical happens when members of a team truly feel

> Two in five Americans sometimes or always feel that their relationships are not meaningful (43 percent) and that they are isolated from others (43 percent).[9]

accepted. When people feel accepted, they feel welcome, and they feel significant. When they feel significant, they open up, lean into their skills and potential, and start crushing their work and life, driving results for their teams and their leaders.

When they make a mistake, remind them their performance doesn't define them. Let them know you trust and believe in them. Remind them how when they bounce back, they'll absolutely continue revealing their character, which is why you hired them.

Everyone *Feels* Accepted at Kimpton

Perhaps one of the greatest examples of an *accepting culture* is Kimpton Hotels and Resorts. At Kimpton, everyone is encouraged to "be your real self." They trust people to do what they do, how they're comfortable doing it. Above all else, *individuality is* at the core of their company culture. Whether an employee works as a valet, front desk cashier, bartender, or department head, Kimpton Hotels wants their people to be themselves.

In fact, they expect it.

When Bill Kimpton started the company as the first boutique hotel company in the United States, he had a vision for this culture and overarching *feel* to their hotels. In chapter 3, I'll introduce to you the concept of the human leader versus the superhuman leader. Though he is no longer with us, Mr. Kimpton is remembered for the way he exemplified the characteristics of a human leader. According to the company's website, the idea behind the first Kimpton hotel was simple: it should be "a place one could stay that felt more like a beautiful, livable, and stylish home rather than a big, impersonal hotel."[10]

The company has continued attracting great talent while sustaining impressive results and significant growth for over three decades.

Each Kimpton hotel experience is unique and different largely because they rely upon and trust their employees to be themselves, adding their own unique spin on service.

Companies often have rules and guidelines that prevent employees from having a unique hair color or cut, or visible piercings or tattoos. Those are usually the same companies that write their people up and discipline them for stepping too far outside the lines or the scripts that they demand their employees deliver. (And then they wonder why half of their workforce is actively looking for jobs elsewhere.)

Not at Kimpton.

At Kimpton, everyone who works there feels *accepted* for who they are. If you ever visit one of their properties, you'll feel the same as a guest. You'll likely be back, time and again.

It's safe to say Bill Kimpton *changed the hotel game* with this culture and his style as a human leader. The company continues doing so today, with game changers who feel *accepted*. So what's the impact of having teams upon teams of people *feeling accepted* for who they are and *feeling encouraged* to lean into their own uniqueness?

Glad you asked.

Their website proudly states, and as you engage in conversation with them, Kimpton employees will likely share some of their success over the years:

- *Fortune* magazine's Best Companies to Work For list nine times
- Featured in Glassdoor Best Place to Work category
- The only hotel and restaurant company to earn a perfect score on the Human Rights Campaign's Corporate Equality Index, year after year

It's not only making a difference for Kimpton's employees—it carries over for their guests. The organization has also been honored as

"Highest in Guest Satisfaction Among Upscale Hotel Chains" by J.D. Power—*three times.*

How Times Have Changed

In 2015, Intercontinental Hotels Group (IHG), the parent company to massive hotel chain Holiday Inn, among other hotel brands, acquired Kimpton Hotels.[11] Holiday Inn used to pride itself on a uniform, one-size-fits-all sea of sameness across all their hotels. In the 1970s, Holiday Inn's tagline was "The best surprise is no surprise." This was their entire brand essence. Their standards were not only set high for their employees, but they were also set in stone. Nobody could venture outside the lines. Everyone had to fit a mold, even if that meant trying to be someone they weren't.

I use this story to illustrate how far we've come and what people—employees as well as customers—expect, value, and appreciate in today's corporate landscape.

Today, employees want to feel welcome enough to be themselves at work. Guests, customers, clients, and key stakeholders also want to be accepted for who they are. Most importantly, they want to feel welcome where they do business. IHG recognized this and appreciated Kimpton's ability to *accept people*—both employees and guests—for who they are. But they also valued the experience they create for everyone with a culture of *acceptance.*

Accept Yourself—But Strive for Self-Mastery

How do leaders leading with hospitality make their teams feel accepted? The answers are simple, but not always easy. Surprisingly, if you're going to accept others, it starts with accepting yourself. After all, if you don't accept who you are, it's very difficult to accept others. That said, accepting yourself is *not* a license to slack off as a leader and say, "It's just who I am."

Take an inventory of your strengths, weaknesses, opportunities, and threats (your emotional triggers that knock you off your game). Become more self-aware of what makes you *you*. A good way to do this is through personality assessments and feedback from your leaders, peers, friends, and family members. The more self-aware you are, the more you'll relax and lean into your uniqueness. You'll be more open, inclusive, and welcoming to your leaders, peers, and especially your employees' distinctive talents, qualities, and uniqueness.

In a book about leading other people with a heart for hospitality, particularly with a focus on them as opposed to on ourselves, the term *self-mastery* may sound counterintuitive. However, before we can become successful leading others, ultimately inspiring them to become the best versions of themselves, we have to commit to that same journey of self-mastery in our own lives.

Striving for self-mastery reminds me of one of the coolest things Walt Disney ever said. Just before Disneyland opened in 1955, Walt was quoted as saying, "Disneyland will never be completed. It will continue to grow as long as there is imagination left in the world." Clearly, since 1955, we've been blessed with everything the Walt Disney Company has given us in the way of memorable experiences in theme parks, resorts, and the inspirational stories that make their full-length animated motion pictures so magical.

The same is true for you and me. Our leadership journey, and even at a higher level, our journey toward self-mastery in our lives will never be completed. We'll never be perfect, but we can continue to learn, grow, and develop into the very best version of ourselves. Your journey has the potential not only to inspire you but also to inspire those you lead. When they see you striving for self-mastery, becoming the best you can possibly be, they'll follow suit.

Self-mastery begins with accepting where you are today, which is always the foundation upon which to build your masterpiece every single day. At the end of each day, ask yourself two questions:

+ What did I do well today?
+ What can I do better tomorrow?

Accept Organizational Realities

When you're the CEO, you get to make policies that affect your entire organization. However, as leaders, we have to acknowledge that we only have power over so much. When you run into a challenge, take time to ask: Is this coming from within my team? From higher up in the company? Is it from outside influences?

We've talked about the value of *accepting who you are* as well as the value of *accepting others for who they are*. Now, let's briefly talk about the power of *accepting organizational realities*.

When speaking to clients, audiences, or leaders attending my leadership workshops, I often prompt the audience, "Raise your hand if you're absolutely ecstatic about every single decision your senior leaders make and you agree with 100 percent of the things the organization is doing 100 percent of the time."

Tongue in cheek, as this is meant to add some levity to an otherwise stressful topic, I pause dramatically so the audience can see that very few people (if any) have raised their hands.

Then I give them another prompt. "Now raise your hand if, in the last week, you've either been so frustrated or so upset about something that happened at work that you spent one, two, or three phone calls or conversations with your friends, family, or coworkers talking about your frustrations with the boss, corporate red tape, or 'him' or 'her' who is on your last nerve."

At this point, everyone is laughing and raising their hands in solidarity with one another.

"Most of us! This is usually the case," I point out as I group myself into that same camp.

I then throw out one more rhetorical question to my new friends in the audience. "But did all those conversations and phone calls and hours spent being frustrated add any value to your situation, solve any problems, or save the world?"

By this time, we're all on the same page.

Everyone relates to this scenario because if there's one thing in life we can be sure of, it's that some things are simply out of our control. There will be people we cannot change, despite how badly they may need to improve, personally or professionally. There will be situations and circumstances that while they may not be ideal nor remain the case over the long term, they are "this" way today.

The temptation is to let all the things we cannot control consume our every thought, conversation, and ounce of being. However, as we've all experienced, that's simply nonproductive. Great leaders challenge themselves and others to *accept what they cannot control* as realities and then quickly shift their thoughts to things they can control.

Imagine all the time, energy, and mental capacity we waste when we worry, obsess about, and pontificate on all the things we can't control. Now imagine how much more productive, positive, and inspired we could be when we focus all our energy on what we have the capacity and ability to change. Most importantly, imagine how inspired others will be when they see us shifting our focus from what we can't control to what we can.

Things we cannot control

- economy
- organizational or corporate politics
- budget cuts or constraints
- leadership or organizational restructuring

Things we can control

- our attitudes
- our efforts
- our mindsets
- our performances

Determine what you can control versus what you cannot. Distinguish between issues stemming from inside your team or organization versus those coming from outside. Why is this important? It will help keep your emotions in check, so you'll be able to listen to, observe, and stay attuned to the emotions of those on your team.

As the leader goes, so goes the team. If you are stressed and emotional, your team will easily become stressed and emotional, distracting them from performing at their highest potential.

Understanding organizational realities helps you focus your mental capacity and energy on more productive, actionable, and winnable battles. Be diligent. Ask questions. Seek to understand, and soon, you'll accept organizational realities that, in turn, help you decide if certain issues are "hills worth dying on."

If you struggle with this, don't worry. You're not alone. I struggle with it just the same as you. But it used to be worse, until I had a leader and mentor of mine earlier in my career pull me aside and take me for a walk. He taught me the concept of *accepting organizational realities* and gave me some hope for how to manage my own thoughts and emotions that caused me to be overly negative too much of the time. It was a lesson I'll never forget and one that I certainly did not want to miss in what I'm now passing on to you.

Now in my work as a speaker and leadership-development consultant, I teach other leaders the power of emotional intelligence. Emotional intelligence (EQ) is the ability to recognize and manage your own thoughts and feelings as well as thoughts and feelings of others. The four components of emotional intelligence will set you apart from the pack, and help you stand out in a crowd (in a *good* way).

The coolest thing about emotional intelligence is that, unlike IQ, our *intelligence quotient,* which is for the most part set by the time we are six and seven years old, our emotional intelligence (EQ) can be improved over time. Each of the four components are woven intricately throughout this entire book, mindset, and lifestyle of *leading with hospitality.*

- **Self-awareness** includes emotional self-awareness, which is being aware of our emotions; an accurate self-assessment, which is fully understanding our strengths; and self-confidence, which of course, is to lean in to who you are and what you're capable of. *Understanding and accepting yourself for who you are.*
- **Self-management** is how you control and manage yourself, your emotions, and your abilities. This includes your ability to manage impulses and focus on more important priorities and goals. In short, a person who's strong in self-management is not easily knocked off track by adversity, tense situations, or stressful times. *Understanding and accepting organizational realities, so you can focus your time, energy, and passions on things you can control, keeping you in a positive rather than negative frame of mind.*

+ **Social awareness** is your ability to recognize the moods, behaviors, and dispositions of those around you and the ability to deploy empathy as you seek to understand how others feel. *This is empathy, one of the most critical leadership skills of all, which we'll unpack in chapter 3, coming right up.*

+ **Relationship management** is your ability to be self-aware of your own emotions and socially aware of others' emotions to manage interactions successfully. These skills are the building blocks to cultivate strong, effective professional relationships. *We unpack the art and science of first building your relationships so that you can eventually "play the orchestra," as Steve Jobs once said. You'll be able to create an engaged team that works well together, with intention and purpose because of your service and inspirational coaching,* which we'll unpack in the balance of this book.

You may be thinking that many of the principles and virtues of leading with hospitality fall under the *relationship management* category. You're right. To create sustainable, positive change in your team or organization's culture, relationships will be the most important thing. The best leaders understand that to deliver great results, they first must foster a culture of great relationships up, down, across, all the way through their organization.

Put *Hospitality in Action*— Activating Acceptance

1. **Accept yourself.** Before you can accept others for who they are, you must accept yourself for who you are. Teams and employees will follow your lead, and they'll begin accepting themselves the more they see you doing the same.

2. **Accept others.** Be inclusive. Despite their quirks, habits, and hang-ups, a leader who leads with hospitality spends time seeking to understand everyone. They look for ways to leverage the value each person brings to the table. Meet people where they are, accepting them for who they are rather than for their accomplishments. When they know you accept them *for them*, they'll slowly but surely feel more welcome with you, on your team, and most importantly, *in their own skin*. That's when they'll lean in, step up, and deliver excellent effort and results for you.

3. **Accept organizational realities.** Determine what you can control versus what you cannot. Separate issues stemming from inside your team or organization versus those coming from outside influences. Be diligent. Ask questions. Seek to understand, and soon, you'll accept organizational realities that, in turn, help you decide if some issues are truly hills worth dying on.

Action Plan to Lead with Hospitality:

CONNECT

*Connect with your team on a human level, and
you'll lead them to the next level.*

We have now reached the end of Part One—CONNECT. At the end
of each part of this book, you will find some helpful prompts and exercises to start leading with hospitality right away. If you like, you can
write in this book. Or grab a notebook or fire up your computer and
open up a new document. Let's get started!

**Connect with each individual on your team by scheduling weekly
one-on-one meetings.** But don't waste your team member's time by
going in unprepared; be genuinely interested in learning more about
them with questions ready to go to keep your conversation flowing.

Here are some examples of great questions to ask as you get to
know your team members on a more personal level:

- What do you like to do in your free time? What are your
  hobbies?
- How do you feel your work/life balance is right now?
- What's one thing we could change about work for you that
  would improve your personal life?

- What part of your job do you enjoy doing most? Why do you enjoy it?
- What have your past managers done that you'd like me to also do or not do?
- What are your career goals and where did your last manager leave off with them?
- What's something you do regularly outside of work that's really important to you?
- What could I do as a manager to make your work easier?
- What's an area of your work you want to improve?
- Who would you like to work with more frequently? Why?
- What part of your job do you wish you didn't have to do?
- What work are you doing here that you feel is most in line with your long-term goals?
- What are your long-term goals? Have you thought about them?
- Could you see yourself making progress on more of your goals here? What would need to change?

Questions for your one-on-one meetings

_____

_____

_____

_____

_____

Connect employees to each other and establish who will do what by when with productive team meetings.

Plan ahead for your team meetings

+ *Define your reason for the meeting (why).*
+ *Define your route or your process for the meeting (how).*
+ *Define the results or your desired outcomes for the meeting (what).*
  − Have an agenda with times for each topic.
  − Establish roles for the meeting.
  − Have fun: be serious about the topics without taking yourself too seriously.
  − Assign who will do what and by when.
  − Finish on time with a roundtable, allowing everyone to share what's on their minds, what stood out for them in the meeting, or the immediate action steps they'll take following the meeting.

Connect your team emotionally to your brand, mission, and cause with written communication, conversations, stories, and experiences.

Define your organization's vision and mission and tell the story consistently across multiple mediums—conversations, your emails, in meetings, and especially one-on-one with your people.

Accept yourself for who you are, accept others for who they are instead of what they've accomplished, and accept organizational realities. You'll be in a more productive and positive mindset to serve your employees to become their best so that you lead your organization to deliver its best results possible.

List your top five strengths and how they will help you achieve your personal and professional goals.

Your Strengths	Your Personal and Professional Aspirations	How Your Strengths Will Help You Achieve Your Aspirations
Example: *Strategic thinker*	*Become a senior executive or start my own business*	My ability to think strategically now will help me practice the future today. I can practice analyzing situations, asking great questions, and over time, I'll become noticed and known as someone capable of growing into an executive role. And I'll further develop my entrepreneurial thinking along the way.

List three people on your team and three of their best characteristics. Challenge yourself to focus on and leverage what they do well as opposed to dwelling on their shortcomings.

Team Member Name	Three of Their Best Characteristics

List one frustrating thing about your organization and challenge yourself to come up with three positive ways to shift your mindset to a more productive place, focusing on what you can control as opposed to what you cannot control.

_____

_____

_____

_____

PART TWO

SERVE

Chapter 3

EMPATHY

Understanding Before Explanation Wins Over Hearts and Minds

Leadership is about empathy. It is about having the ability to relate to and connect with people for the purpose of inspiring and empowering their lives.

—Oprah Winfrey

In February 2016, in the locker room at halftime, Steve Kerr, the head coach of the Golden State Warriors, and his superstar, Draymond Green, nearly came to blows. A professional basketball player and his coach almost fought each other. Kerr called Green out, and by all accounts, Green immediately went ballistic. Despite the yelling, profanity, threats, and heaven knows what else, the fight didn't become physical. It was a dark moment, but it proved to be significant.

It was the beginning of two headstrong competitors finally coming to understand one another.

Nearly a year later, the Warriors were dominating the NBA. They'd won forty-nine of their first fifty-eight games. However, the always vocal Green was in a funk, playing poorly, and speaking about "the brand of basketball" Kerr had the team playing. An article from Bleacher Report tells how Kerr took Green out of a game with ten minutes remaining, letting him watch from the bench. It was Kerr's way of saying, "Maybe we shouldn't talk right now."

What happens next is an amazing illustration of *leadership empathy*.

According to the Bleacher Report article (and other accounts), Kerr wrote Green a three-page letter. The first line said, "I love you and respect you. I know you are hurting. We need to talk."[12]

Green told the media that after reading the first three sentences, he threw the letter away. Those opening lines told him everything he needed to know. Green told the media that at that moment, he felt Kerr, with whom he often clashed, truly understood him.

Green said, "He gets me. I'm good. Whatever anger was built up inside is gone!" Sure, the Golden State Warriors had phenoms Steph Curry and Klay Thompson, along with Andrea Iguodala, Shaun Livingston, and others. However, Kerr knew Green was the heartbeat of the team. His passion, unrivaled basketball IQ, work ethic, talent, and drive made everyone else better.

By Kerr's admission, it wasn't until he *understood* more about what made Green tick that he led the team to new heights. By investing time talking to Green's college coach, Tom Izzo, and to Green himself, Kerr learned to loosen his grip. He began to understand how Green ignited the entire team and what drove his success. Kerr is quoted as saying, "Draymond's made a big impact on me because I've watched him go from a second-round pick, tweener, 'what position does he play?' to All-star. And he's done it with intellect, versatility, and bravado. Without that bravado, Draymond isn't Draymond. So, who am I to tell somebody, 'Hey, don't! Tone it back!' When maybe toning it up is what might help you become great."

That same Bleacher Report article quoted Green as saying, "It's amazing to know someone thinks that of you, especially your coach, who's meant so much to the game of basketball. I mean, I'm kind of lost for words, because that means a lot to me. Steve Kerr, my relationship with coach, it means a lot. And to know that he kind of thinks that of me and views me like that, it really means a lot."

As I write this, the Kerr and Green connection has led the Warriors to three NBA titles in four years. Their relationship is a special one, as they continue communicating every day, whether in or out of season, on game days as well as off nights.

Green would run headfirst into a brick wall for Kerr. He loves and appreciates his coach, leader, and boss, because he knows Kerr *understands* him.

According to Businessolver's 2020 State of Workplace Empathy Report, 83 percent of employees would consider leaving their current organization for a similar role at a more empathetic organization. And 74 percent of employees said they would work longer hours for an empathetic employer.[13]

Kerr leads with hospitality in many ways, but perhaps mostly by having empathy. He continues investing time to understand what's happening inside the hearts and minds of his players.

Leadership Empathy

Empathy is a great way to anticipate needs to deliver impeccable service. It's a special leadership trait rarely practiced enough. The HR technology company Businessolver has published their State of Workplace Empathy research report yearly since 2016; as they have consistently found, "Employees feel as though their leaders are not doing enough to display empathy."[14] And most people surveyed would consider leaving their current job for a similar one at a more empathetic organization.

What does this mean? People don't leave their jobs. They leave their leaders. Despite the many differences you may see between you and those you lead, remember that all of us have one thing in common: we're all human beings. As humans, we're wired to connect, be social, and form relationships. If we don't find what we need in one place, we go looking for it someplace else. The people on our teams are no different. If they don't *feel* a connection or a human relationship with their boss, their priorities shift from leaning into performing well at their job to looking for a new one every night when they go home.

Human connection that leads to meaningful relationships and strong bonds begins with understanding one another. That's the magic of empathy. Empathy isn't necessarily agreeing with the other person. It's simply the ability to understand how the other person is feeling. Everything changes when we, as social beings longing for connection and relationship at work just as much as at home, know someone understands us.

When leaders embody the meaningful and powerful leadership skill, empathy, their teams feel welcome. They're also moved to move. Big, bad, and bold, Draymond Green is a six-and-a-half-feet tall power forward. He's one of the most intimidating competitors ever to play in the NBA. But his coach's empathy moves him on the inside, which propels him to deliver for the team on the outside.

The same will be true with your team when you add empathy to your leadership toolkit and leverage it to make sure your teams feel welcome. Remember: you hired them because of who they are; if you lead with hospitality, as we discussed in chapter 2, you make sure your team knows they're *accepted* for who they are. This ignites their feelings of significance, which sparks their highest levels of productivity, not to mention creates reasons for them to stay with you and your organization over the long haul. Turnover is costly, and it can become one of your biggest roadblocks to creating or changing the culture where you work.

The research tells us that people will leave us at alarming rates just to go work for a more empathetic boss, and they're telling us that they'll work harder and longer hours if only their boss would show a little more empathy. If you're a numbers person, then there is your justification to lean into your humanness and show those you lead some empathy. But one thing I know about you is that you too are human. So you know that empathy is just the right thing to do. And as Martin Luther King Jr. said, "The time is always right to do what's right."

A Tale of Two Leaders: The Superhuman Leader versus the Human Leader

Before I get into how you can show empathy to the people on your team, I want to talk about how *not* to do this. In my work, I often see two types of leaders, the superhuman leader and the human leader. On your career journey, you may have experienced them both.

The superhuman leader tells you stories about how unbelievably awesome they are and how bad they used to have it. Ultimately, they unleashed their superhuman powers to overcome adversity and make everything perfect because, well, they are awesome. They share stories of how successful they've become, how much money they have, and how big their house is. Also, in true "superhuman fashion," you never hear them talk about when they've fallen short of the mark. They've never been wrong, and they never made mistakes. They basically have no faults because they possess all six Infinity Stones. They're superhuman!

The human leader, on the other hand, shares lessons they learned the hard way, having made mistakes along their journey. They ask more discovery questions to learn about others because they genuinely care. They know they're not perfect. They don't hide the fact that they're a work in progress. Human leaders tell stories of tough seasons when things were falling apart, but they always share what they learned during those storms. They pass along nuggets they've learned from their leaders, usually giving them credit for their own growth.

Human leaders come out and tell the people the two most welcoming words in the English language, "I understand."

The difference in the superhuman leader and human leader is a feeling of being understood. When a superhuman leader tells his or her story of perfection and superpowers, about zero out of ten people will relate or feel what they share is relevant. Because here on planet Earth, nobody is perfect. Since they're not relatable, few people are in a big hurry to enthusiastically follow a superhuman leader.

Conversely, when the human leader tells his or her story of imperfection and being *human*, ten out of ten people relate. Everyone's drawn toward a humbler human leader. They ask more questions because they want to know and learn more from them.

Which type of leader would you follow? More importantly, which type of leader do you want to be?

Why?

We. Are. All. Human.

It's all about finding common ground. The quicker you find it, the quicker you'll relate. And the more quickly you relate, the more you'll solidify the emotional connections with your team. As we know from Jonathan Haidt's famous elephant-and-rider analogy, to move people to move, we must "motivate the elephant." That is to say, once again, before anyone becomes inspired to *do* anything, they must first *feel*. Deploying empathy is the most impactful, human way to establish and leverage emotional connections with those you lead.

Genuine empathy means seeking to understand and putting yourself in their shoes. It's also about relating to their situation, how they feel, and helping them come out on the other side of a stormy season a stronger human than before.

Show empathy with your team and every person in your life. That's leading with hospitality at its finest, its purest, and in its most meaningful form.

Seek Understanding

Empathy is about understanding, not necessarily agreeing. Volumes of research have been written and published about the productive nature of agreeing to disagree. (For a great resource, *Harvard Business Review*'s contributing editor, Amy Gallo, published an insightful, research-based HBR article in January 2018 entitled "Why We Should Be Disagreeing More at Work."[15]) Often, the dialogue itself is healthy, because on the other side, both people understand even if they see things differently.

Why is this impactful?

Without understanding, it's amazing what we can conjure up in our minds about what another person thinks or feels. This gap in understanding drives a wedge deeper and prevents relationships from sprouting and blossoming. When understanding gaps exist, productivity lags, culture change is impossible, and results continue to come in south of expectations.

Seek to understand even if you disagree. Taking the time to understand builds your credibility in the eyes of your team. It makes you human and more relatable, and most importantly, it gradually leads to trust and respect.

We're quick to jump right into solving or fixing issues. It's human nature; not to mention a very natural inclination to anyone in a leadership position. We think, since we're the ones with the title or with the responsibility, we have to be all-knowing all the time. Those who lead with hospitality know enough to know what they don't know, and they understand there are things they don't understand. Most importantly, they view challenges as opportunities, breakdowns in processes, and disconnects between and among members of the team as opportunities to improve.

Before you jump into fixing mode, spend some time seeking to understand. For example, simply ask things like the following:

- What's getting in your way?
- How are your relationships with person X or Y?
- Can you help me understand why you feel this way?
- Which direction would you rather go and why would that work better?
- How can we reach a compromise, with a solution that works for both of us?

You'll learn more details and gain more knowledge about the situation. While this does take a little extra time and thoughtfulness, consider it a proverbial deposit into the trust-and-respect bank in the eyes of those you lead. When they see you taking the time to understand their specific situation, you become more credible, more trustworthy, and someone worth following.

If you don't seek to understand, you become just like every other boss, manager, or so-called leader who barks out orders. Few want to follow that type of leader for very long. So they usually don't.

Vocalize Your Understanding

Seeking to understand is half the battle. The next step, and possibly the most important to the person you're leading, is to actually say you understand.

When you choose the path of the human leader as opposed to the superhuman leader, people feel it. The overwhelmingly welcome feelings of acceptance lead to significance. As they feel more significant, when they know you understand, the relationship goes to the next level. That relationship brings next-level emotions of credibility, respect, and trust.

These are the simple ingredients for engaging in new, meaningful ways of working, changing culture, and delivering next-level results with next-level productivity. If we want to drive next-level results, we first have to take our humanness to the next level. One of the most human things a leader at any level can do is to admit fault or simply share when they've learned something new. While many will take the step to seek to understand, it takes next-level humanness and humility to tell someone else the extent to which you truly understand their situation, challenge, or predicament.

Conventional wisdom—and I use the word *wisdom* lightly— may suggest that letting others know the extent to which we may not have known or understood something is a sign of weakness. Leaders who lead with hospitality understand that appearing weak is far less important than establishing human connections with those they lead. The humanness and humility it takes to pause, seek to understand, and then ultimately share your understanding makes for strong emotional connections.

Those emotional connections ultimately become the driving force behind new, elevated realms of passion, productivity, and purpose when those you lead understand just how much you really do understand how they feel about their current situation.

Few leadership tools, tactics, or skills are as impactful as empathy. When they know you understand, your relationships will grow deep roots. As any gardener will tell you, the stronger the root, the more plentiful the fruit. Here are some statements you can use to convey how much you truly understand:

- If I had experienced what you just experienced, I'd be just as frustrated (or tired or upset or angry or disappointed) as you.
- It makes me really upset to hear this happened.
- I appreciate your trusting me with this—it means a lot.
- I sense some of these new processes and changes are becoming stressful. I'm right there with you. Let's chat about how we can get more comfortable being uncomfortable as we go through this together.

Empathy is the bedrock of service, and service is the bedrock of leadership.

Be Willing to Adapt

How often have we seen iconic hotels, resorts, and restaurants change course and "refurbish for our future enjoyment"? It happens often.

Hotels reconstruct rooms, pool decks, lobbies, and meeting spaces to stay relevant for their guests, customers, and clients. Restaurants change and modify menu items, furniture, equipment, and even reinvent their reservation systems.

Why?

They've invested time engaging with guests to understand what they like and dislike and what would make them feel more welcome. They care enough about their relationship and the future of their business to adapt how they serve up their products, services, and experiences.

Leading with hospitality follows this sentiment. As a leader, continually ask how you should adapt to better serve your teams. And then follow through on what you hear. Be willing to alter your policies, change workflows and processes, or respond differently, or be prepared to explain to them why things can't change right now.

When you take the time to unleash compassion and practice empathy, you'll discover the attributes and characteristics of your most important asset, your people.

Just as Steve Kerr learned how to best leverage and channel Draymond Green's quirks, you can do the same with your teams. While you may have set out in one direction, with a certain tone, cadence, or dialogue, it's okay to adapt and change. You can change the subject, based upon what resonates best with your team. Once you learn and understand what motivates and drives people, modify and adapt your leadership game plan accordingly.

You'll build trust and credibility like never before. Your people will feel welcome. You'll be on your way to delivering for your senior leaders—changing the culture, transforming groups of people into high-performing teams, and delivering results.

Put *Hospitality in Action*— Activating Empathy

1. **Seek to understand.** Carve out and plan quality time with each person on your team. Chances are, few leaders have done this. When they realize you intentionally blocked out time for them, you'll enjoy new realms of trust and credibility.

   Pull; don't push. Ask purposeful questions with genuine interest to understand situations, sentiments, and challenges. Focus on seeking to understand versus driving home your points. Only then will you see and feel communication break-throughs with individuals and the team as a group.

2. **Share your understanding.** You're human, not superhuman. So connect with people on a human level, and you'll take your team to the next level. Simply share how much you do understand how they feel, what's in their way, where they want to go in their lives and careers, and why they do what they do or believe what they believe.

3. **Show that you understand.** Show them; don't tell them. You've heard the cliché, "Talk is cheap." Not only has your team heard it, but also they've experienced it firsthand, from past leaders. They will know you're different when you put empathy and understanding into action with the decisions you make and changes you implement.

   Adapt or die. Nothing will demoralize a team more than a leader who is adamant about "doing it the way we've always done it." Conversely, few actions will lift them up, give them hope, and ignite productivity more than a dynamic, human leader who's not afraid to adjust and innovate to new ways of working.

Chapter 4

SERVICE

To Serve Is to LEAD—
Listen, Educate, Act, Deliver

*Success isn't about how much money you make; it's about the
difference you make in people's lives.*

—Michelle Obama

I n chapter 1, I mentioned my first full-time leadership role out of
college as a housekeeping manager for the opening of Gaylord
Palms Resort and Convention Center, in Kissimmee, Florida. I
started back in February 2002.

It was very nearly the job I never had.

The tragic events of September 11, 2001, had impacted seemingly
everyone across the world in many unfortunate ways. The job market,
especially in the travel industry, was hit hard during that time. Hotels
were laying off employees, cutting pay, and barely keeping the lights on,
as travel everywhere came to a screeching halt.

Yet a beacon of hospitality light during this dark time was Gaylord Palms Resort and Convention Center. They were new, a breath of fresh air in the meeting-and-convention business—and they'd go on to change the game in the industry with grandiose atriums in the lobby, hundreds of thousands of square feet of meeting-and-convention space, and world-class dining experiences with legendary service. Experiences at this scale were seldom found outside of Las Vegas or Walt Disney World in those days. Gaylord disrupted the space as they went on to open Gaylord National, near Washington, DC; Gaylord Texan, near Dallas, Texas; and Gaylord Rockies, near Denver, Colorado. At the time, though, one of their most attractive qualities was . . . they were hiring! That was the good news. The bad news was that thousands upon thousands of highly qualified people in central Florida and other parts of the country applied to work there.

They held a grand-hire event, an all-nighter where hiring leaders literally wore pajamas to conduct interviews from 7:00 PM to 7:00 AM the next morning. I was finishing up a temporary management internship at Disney's Contemporary Resort, but obviously I needed a full-time job after the end of my program.

The following morning, I was scheduled to be the opening manager at the front desk of Disney's Contemporary Resort, with a 7:00 AM start time. My plan was to show up at the grand-hire event at Gaylord Palms in my suit and tie at 4:00 AM, hopefully get noticed, interview, and then make it to my 7:00 AM front-desk-manager shift with no problem.

At 4:00 AM, I pulled into a sea of cars and people in the parking lot. I remember thinking everyone south of Atlanta must have driven to Kissimmee for this event. The place was *packed*, and we all needed jobs. I finally found a spot, parked, and approached the front doors where I noticed a few people exiting, but nobody entering.

Just before making it to the entrance doors, I noticed someone was turned away. The employee manning the door told her to apply online. I realized they weren't letting anyone else inside. I didn't make eye contact, turned on a dime, and walked around to the side of the building to try to find another way inside. Now, it was like a game. I wasn't leaving until I at least had a chance to interview. I was there in a suit and tie at 4:00 AM after all—I was invested.

At the next set of doors, I pressed my nose against the glass and peeked inside. Not a soul. But the door was unlocked. I walked in with a confident stride like I was already a general manager and went looking for someone to hire me.

At about 4:15 AM, I met Ralph Larsen, the executive housekeeper, and Dave Chylinski, director of housekeeping. Their first question was, "How did you get in here? We stopped letting people in an hour ago."

"I walked in the side door," I replied. After they stopped laughing, we had a nice conversation about why I wanted to be a housekeeping manager at their new gem of a hotel. I don't remember everything about the interview, but I remember our conversation about serving people. They explained what they were looking for, the type of work it entailed, and what I needed to do for them to be successful.

I liked what I heard, appreciated their time meeting with me that early in the morning, and I was honest. I told them I made the decision to major in hospitality in college and work in the industry because I loved everything about hospitality. My favorite part was being of service.

Thankfully, they noticed me and chose me.

Beyond the personal connections, I remember appreciating how they served the entire team and me in my role as a young, first-time manager.

It was a mega-resort hotel opening with 3.2 acres, four hundred thousand square feet of meeting-and-convention space, three full-service restaurants, a café, two bars, and 1,406 rooms. We were the housekeeping team, tasked with overseeing the upkeep, cleaning, and refreshing of the rooms and common areas. However, in a hotel-opening situation, nothing is put together when you show up for the job. It's the most overwhelming, yet unbelievably rewarding feeling to open a hotel, largely because of the teamwork required to pull it off—and, for us managers, lots of project work, hiring staff, training teams, and literally putting together the puzzle that would soon be introduced to the world as Orlando's next game-changing resort.

We planned to open to guests on February 2, 2002 (02-02-02), at 2:02 PM. I remember it was mid-January, and Ralph, Dave, and I stood in the property's exhibit hall, speechless. The massive space would soon be home to huge conventions, trade shows, and special events. At the time, though, it was still the preopening season. So there were no guests yet. At this moment, it was the staging area for every single item that would decorate, outfit, and stock the resort. The contents of 1,406 guestrooms were still in boxes in the exhibit hall. This included every pillow, pillowcase, all the linens, clock radios, shower hooks, shower curtains, telephones, notepads, pens, shampoo, soap, body wash, conditioner, body lotion, right down to those fancy little stickers you find on the toilet paper upon check-in when you enter your guestroom for the first time.

To imagine what this felt like, think of being in a cornfield in Iowa where as far as the eye can see, it's nothing but rows of corn. Got it? Okay, now imagine that instead of corn, there are endless rows of boxes. Box after box of clock radios, pillows, blankets, bedding, and so on. You get the picture. It was approximately a half-mile walk, by way of underground tunnels, to the service elevators that eventually led to the guestrooms. It was about 4:00 PM, and we'd already been working since six o'clock that morning.

One of the senior leaders of the resort walked into the exhibit hall as Ralph, Dave, and I were still surveying, thinking about how we would somehow pull this off by 2:02 PM on February 2 for our grand-opening celebration (which was awesome, by the way; fireworks in the atrium, the whole nine yards). The senior leader who walked up to us that afternoon also took in the "field" of boxes upon boxes. He said, with executive presence and confidence, "You guys have a lot of work to do."

All we could do was laugh. All four of us.

His delivery was a little tongue-in-cheek, but his statement was true. We had a lot of work to do.

Here's why I tell that story: Dave and Ralph embodied service in the context of leading with hospitality. What happened over the next two weeks was nothing short of amazing. Executive Housekeeper Ralph and Director of Housekeeping Dave had eleven of us, front-line leaders in housekeeping, plus over 150 frontline housekeepers and housemen. They could have easily rolled the carts over to me, their twenty-two-years-young first-time manager and left me to figure it out. They could have easily pulled rank and deemed themselves "above" the tasks at hand.

They didn't do that.

In fact, they did just the opposite. Ralph, Dave, and I, along with the rest of our team, sat down and strategically devised a plan for how in the world we would get every little accessory and trinket from this exhibit hall into these 1,406 guestrooms before the moment we flung the doors open to guests. We did it together. They were right there in the mix with me and everyone else.

For the next two weeks, everyone knew who did what and by when, each day. We each took a team of our staff, and item by item, cart by cart, and shower hook by shower hook, we got to work.

On any given hour of any day during that two weeks, you'd find Ralph and Dave actively participating in all the work being completed. They pushed carts, carried boxes, plugged in clock radios, programmed said clock radios, and they didn't stop there.

See, I was fresh out of college, single, and at the time living four-wide in an apartment (it could have been the Orlando 2002 version of MTV's *The Jersey Shore*). So, aside from being at a bar with friends or at the pool, I had few places to go or anywhere else to be but Gaylord Palms Resort and Convention Center. I told Ralph he could feel free to count on me to stay late and come in early anytime. Since they were so invested to serve me and the rest of the team, I was inspired to do whatever it took to get this resort open, on time and on budget.

He took me up on it, but he also came in with me. He was married with a beautiful young daughter and wife at home. He came in early and stayed late anyway. We prepared cleaning chemicals for our housekeeping team together, we stocked rooms together, we organized housekeeping carts together, unpacked boxes side by side, and carted the contents to their destination, over and over.

He served.

He and Dave served me so much. Their presence alone, and the spirit with which they led us and served us in that preopening season and beyond, inspired everyone to do more and be more, and to not even think about quitting until the job was finished.

Ralph and Dave both knew I was a huge basketball fan. At one point during our "hotel combine" of sorts, Dave wanted to show his appreciation for our hard work. He arranged for Ralph to take me to an Orlando Magic game. Back then, the Magic had a squad! Tracy McGrady, Mike Miller, Dee Brown, Patrick Ewing, Horace Grant, Grant Hill, and Pat Garrity, to name a few. Plus, Doc Rivers at the helm as the coach. They finished third in the Eastern Conference that year and made the playoffs. It was great basketball: electric, every game. I remember on the way back from the game, Ralph looked at me, and said, "Oh, by the way, we have to do linen inventory when we get back tonight." (That entails literally counting every single towel, washcloth, and sheet of linen in every linen closet on every floor of the resort. It's big fun.)

I cracked up.

"Taylor, I'm not kidding," he said.

I didn't even care. I just said, "No problem. This is awesome!"

The Impact of Serving Your Team

We've all experienced unbelievable service in some way, shape, or form. A great hotel check-in, an incredible dining experience, a bartender with charisma, or perhaps that one call-center representative on the other end of the phone who worked his or her magic to solve a problem, averting what would've been a crisis. Regardless of the type of experience, the impact of their outstanding service left us feeling amazing.

When we receive great service, we feel so incredibly welcome. Beyond that, we feel an overwhelming sense of appreciation. Again, it's almost an emotional thing.

Forgive me for being dramatic; but consider the fact that appreciation is an emotion. And the emotional connection we experience when we enjoy great hospitality creates stories worth repeating. It also creates feelings we want to return to over and over. Plus, it compels us to move and act.

When you serve your team, doing everything you can to help them become better, more successful, more fulfilled, or even more productive, they'll appreciate you. When they appreciate you, they'll give back tenfold. Taking me to an Orlando Magic game may have been one of the smartest leadership moves Ralph and Dave made that season even though I had to go back and work again after the game. They *gave* so much to me, served me and our teams so well, that I *felt* compelled to *give* more of myself to them and for our organization.

Once, during a huge checkout day when we were turning over one thousand guests, I found myself sprinting in one of the tunnels with an armload of towels. A day like that is a battle for the housekeeping manager to coordinate the cleaning of all those rooms so they're ready for the next wave of check-ins in a few hours. Would anyone sprint like that for a boss they didn't appreciate? Maybe. But I doubt it.

> Only 61 percent of people feel a sense of leadership
> —O. C. Tanner Institute, 2020 Global Culture Report[16]

The beautiful thing about serving your team is, even if the job sucks and everyone knows it, the fact that you're still serving them, as human beings, is appreciated. They'll know you appreciate them, and in turn, they'll appreciate you. They'll continue rolling up their sleeves, diving in, and sprinting for you and for the team as long as they know you're still sprinting for them.

How to Serve with LEAD

Serving your team is dynamic. As leaders we can serve people in many ways.

We can also serve in countless ways outside work, at home and in our communities. Here are some simple, yet impactful ways to serve the people on your teams. I like to use an acronym I call **LEAD**: Listen, Educate, Act, and Deliver.

1. Listen

We started talking about listening in chapter 3, "Empathy," but listening is also an integral part of great service.

Listen to your team: When they know you listen, you and your employees will be well served. Your team will appreciate the shoulder, the ear, and the attention. Listening doesn't always mean you must provide a solution. In fact, in most situations, listening is all people need or want. If they want advice, they'll usually ask. Listening is about being present and willing to help. It's the very foundation of service. Then ask purposeful questions with genuine interest to understand situations, sentiments, and challenges. Focus on seeking to understand versus driving home your points.

Listen to your own leaders: Your boss, her boss, and her boss's boss are in their roles for many reasons.

You may be perfectly aware of *why* they're in the role of director, vice president, or chief; other times, you may wonder why. Trust that, to some extent, they've walked in your shoes, which makes them viable resources. Don't be afraid to ask questions and be humble enough to actively *listen* to their advice and guidance. When you actively listen for feedback, and when you implement it, you'll serve your team, your leaders, your organization, and even your community well.

Listen to your guests, customers, and clients: The best brands and best leaders serve people, whether it's overdelivering, creating a memorable experience, or adding value in some way. One of the simplest, yet most frequently missed opportunities to serve is to simply listen. When people take time to share feedback, it's a way of saying they care, as they genuinely hope you'll improve. Listen to your guests, customers, and clients, and you'll create a culture of service.

Listen to your own intuition: If you feel something is off, or a different approach might serve your team better, you're probably on to something. Trust your gut, as they say. Listen to the voices in your head and heart. Those voices are your intuition. They're almost always wise and usually worth exploring. Pay attention to your intuition, and you'll serve your team well, making sure everyone's focused on doing the right thing.

2. Educate

This means taking advantage of teachable moments, not being preachy. Take an extra five minutes here or half an hour there to engage and educate your team. Consider all the times throughout your career when you wish someone educated you instead of leaving you on your own to figure something out. Chances are, few leaders have given the people on your team the attention they need and deserve. Invest time to teach. Your team will feel more welcome and comfortable, and they'll deliver incredible results.

As a leader, look for teachable, coachable moments. Plant seeds in the hearts and minds of people, and you'll serve them today and for a lifetime. You'll lay the foundation today for them to succeed tomorrow.

A few leaders of mine stand out as excellent teachers. Scott was my manager at Disney's Pop Century Resort, and he had a meeting with us the day before we opened that 2,880-room property in 2003. He carved out time to talk to us about teamwork and how to align on processes. But he also made sure we truly believed in the amazing experience we were creating. Like Ralph and Dave, Scott served us every single day— he listened, taught, coached, and certainly chipped in to help. Then, in 2008, at Encore at Wynn Las Vegas, I was on another hotel-opening team, as the director of Red Card, Wynn Resorts' loyalty marketing program. My leader in that experience was Tom, a veteran of Las Vegas hotel openings, who had opened the Bellagio and Wynn Las Vegas in the years before I met him. He was a great planner and teacher. He was all about the details, and paid special attention to teaching me what he had learned from his experiences.

At one point while I was project managing some new signage creation throughout the casino for our department, Tom had me send a vendor back to the drawing board multiple times, just because he wanted the color to match perfectly with other furniture, fixtures, and equipment on the floor. He raised my bar for excellence, and I would go on to raise the bar for others later in my career.

He knew I wanted to learn and grow, so he took the time to meet, walk, and talk with me, and he even called and texted some evenings with encouragement when he felt I needed it. I always appreciated his time and told myself I'd always do my best to give that kind of time to people I led in the future.

3. Act

All talk and no action from leadership is demoralizing for a team. However, backing up a helpful coaching session with specific action steps to drive a team forward is noticed. When you take action, it's not only contagious, it also builds credibility and trust with those you lead.

When you act, your team will act.

Show them; don't tell them. You've heard the cliché "Talk is cheap." Your team has heard it before and experienced it from past leaders. Be different when you put empathy and understanding into action.

Personal accountability: Great leaders go first. That includes taking accountability for the work or tasks at hand. Even when you're entrusted with a leadership position, you must be first to act and move. When you're accountable for what needs to be accomplished, your teams, peers, and sometimes even your own leaders follow suit.

Do: When things go south or when we fall behind, the first question a senior leader will ask is "What are you doing about it?" Be ready to answer that question to whoever asks, including members of your team. Less talking and more doing always serves your team, your organization, and your community.

4. Deliver

Make good on your promises. Nothing makes a person feel welcome on a team like the boss going to bat for them. Whether it's advocating for a team member to executives or the board of directors or cleaning the breakroom to make space for a new Keurig, always serve.

Add as much or more value to their experience as you ask them to add to your guests', clients', or customers' lives. You'll be appreciated for it, and your team will feel amazing as they do great work.

When you first accepted a job as a leader, you made a promise. You promised the people who hired you that you'd take responsibility for everything from the employee experience to the experience you ultimately provide for guests, customers, and clients.

It's about influencing, motivating, and inspiring, which we'll discuss later.

Deliver on your team's expectations: The number one driver of performance is clear expectations. This applies to leaders setting clear expectations for employees. It also applies in the context of how you perform as a leader. Great leaders communicate what they expect to their teams for sure. They also have the courage to ask their teams what they expect of them, as their leader. It takes humility and a heart for hospitality, to approach leadership as a vessel to serve. Delivering on expectations is one of the best ways to provide great service to your team and a surefire way to deliver inspirational leadership.

Deliver MORE: Dolly Parton said, "If your actions create a legacy that inspires others to dream more, learn more, do more, and become more, then, you are an excellent leader."

At The Cosmopolitan of Las Vegas (more on that in the next section), we had a mantra, as we put on a show for our guests, customers, and clients. It was *Give MORE*. MORE was an acronym that stood for *magic, original, relevant,* and *engaging*. It held everyone accountable to *deliver MORE*, and made it easy to remember what we were actually there to deliver.

Here's how to lead with hospitality and deliver MORE.

- *Magic* means create experiences that surprise, delight, or uplift.
- *Original* is about thinking outside the box in new and different ways.
- *Relevant* means ensuring every decision supports and advances the team's mission, bringing the organization's purpose and vision to life.
- *Engaging* refers to enrolling and inviting people to share the best of themselves so we deliver the best experience possible.

To this day, when I look back, The Cosmopolitan of Las Vegas was my favorite career stop along the way. Because it was more than a job. It truly was *meaningful work*. I gave more of myself to people, and I watched as they gave every bit of themselves to me, our guests, each other, and to The Cosmopolitan's mission to completely change the game in Las Vegas.

Deliver MORE. You'll serve in ways you never thought possible, and your team will deliver results they never thought possible.

When You Serve Others, They Pay It Forward

As I said, The Cosmopolitan of Las Vegas was one of my favorite parts of my career. I was blessed in late 2010 to be on the property's opening team. By that time, I had been through several hotel openings—at Gaylord Palms as a housekeeping manager, Disney's Pop Century Resort as a front-desk manager, and Encore at Wynn Las Vegas as a department head. I'd grown to love the day before opening night. It's the final day of preopening, when you can walk through the near-empty hotel, watching everything sparkle. You'll never be in the hotel alone without guests ever again once you open to the public and invite the world to come play. It's a thing of beauty, and when you're on the opening team, it feels like you own a little piece of it and you're about to *gift* it to the world. You feel anxious, excited, nervous, determined, and extremely emotional all at once. The next day, the lights come on, and it's showtime; from that point forward, guests will be in the hotel every single day and every single night.

For The Cosmopolitan's opening, I was the director of a department: as director of membership, I led the loyalty marketing team of roughly forty people. (This was our version of the "player's club," where you join the loyalty program and earn points for spending money in the casino, restaurants, and other retail outlets throughout the resort.) So for me, this opening was a little different than what I'd experienced before as a frontline leader. Luckily for me, I had great leaders like Ralph, Dave, Scott, and Tom as my department heads in the past. They showed me how to serve teams in the years prior, and I was determined to serve my team just as they had served me.

Opening night was December 15, 2010. So naturally, December 14 was somewhat of a marathon day, putting the finishing touches on everything, preparing, and troubleshooting last-minute operational details.

On December 14, we all started our day at 7:00 AM sharp. I held a team meeting, a quick huddle to fire up the team for what we needed to be an efficient, productive, and intense day of last-minute preparation. The message was that we get one chance to make our opening night successful: there's only one opening night, so we have to be great.

I rolled up my sleeves and worked alongside my team just like Ralph and Dave did with me back at Gaylord Palms. I huddled my team up daily in various areas of the hotel lobby, casino, in and around restaurants, and even outside at the pool, and facilitated conversations about teamwork, believing in what we were creating, and aligning on processes just like Scott had done with us back at Disney's Pop Century Resort. I stayed late and came in early, peering over project plans, guest flow sequences, membership booth designs, and especially who would need to do what to ensure flawless execution, just as I learned from Tom back at Wynn and Encore Las Vegas.

We were so fired up. We cruised through the day but found ourselves in a predicament at around eight o'clock at night—thirteen hours after our day had begun, and twenty-four hours before we would open to the public. We still needed to print thousands of membership cards in preparation for thousands of arrivals on opening night. We also realized that we had never received our marketing collateral—brochures, key packets, property maps, and so on. Since we were in the marketing department, it was relatively important for the loyalty marketing program to have marketing collateral on opening night! So needless to say, these were daunting, time-consuming tasks that seemed impossible given our time crunch.

Two of the managers on my team, Tom (yes, another Tom!) and Mike, were still on property with me. We had only known each other for one month at this point, so we had no clue how our warehouse process worked, and barely knew where the warehouse was.

Tom stepped up and said, "I'll take the cards. I know it's late, but we have to get it done." He had been on his feet for fifteen hours, but there was no way he was going home until the job was completed and checked off our list.

He painstakingly printed out card after card after card, at our identity membership booth until midnight. The next night, on opening night, we were prepared to handle the masses. Thousands of guests flooded into the hotel when the doors opened at 8:00 PM, and everyone came right to us for their identity membership cards.

We were ready, all because Tom was committed to serving us as a team and our guests.

Mike stepped up as well. As we brainstormed just how in the world we were going to get twenty-five-plus boxes of marketing collateral from the warehouse (I had no clue where it was or how to get there) to all the various locations throughout the resort where they belonged, Mike said, "Hey, I drive a pickup truck. Why don't we just load it up with our stuff and bring it back here tonight."

That's exactly what we did.

Mike and I saddled up in his truck, backed it up to one of the loading docks at the warehouse, and did our thing, loading box after box into the bed of his truck and taking it all back to the hotel. On opening night, we not only had all of our brochures and collateral at the identity membership booths, but we also picked up enough collateral for our partners in concierge.

This was also Mike's idea.

He wasn't thinking about how long we'd been there that day. He was thinking about serving people. He always called me "Captain." And that day and night, he kept telling me, as the hours wore on, "If you're here, I'm here, Captain. Let's make this opening great!"

I'll remember that night for the rest of my life. It was pretty cool. We had just met a month prior but couldn't stop talking about how much we loved the hotel, the people, and our product. At the time, I remember thinking I was like Tom and Mike nine years prior, serving my team and my leaders because of how much Ralph and Dave served me. Tom said he was inspired to serve us and our guests because of how much I'd been serving him and the rest of our team in the short time we'd been together. It had all come full circle.

That's hospitality and leadership in a nutshell. At the core of both is being of service to people. When you serve people, it makes an impact not only in the moment but also for years to come. It's a chain reaction of inspiration. When you serve others, they become inspired to serve others, and on and on, the story goes.

Get in the Sauce

In my first year as a consultant, one of my first clients was a four-diamond hotel in Louisville, Kentucky. The general manager who hired me gave me clear direction and expectations. He said, "I want you in the sauce," and with the people. He wanted me in conversations, asking questions, listening, observing, and *serving* them just as much or more as we were serving our guests.

My role was to teach and coach several new leaders and employees recently brought on board and help the executive team streamline processes while enhancing experiences for guests and staff. *Getting in the sauce* was the best way to learn, connect, and help. It was also the best way to serve. I served everything from food to valet and bell services, while also serving employees, new leaders starting on their journey, and delivering a service to my client, the general manager.

The only way I could deliver great service was to *get in the sauce*. It's the same for you, as a leader. When you're with your team every step of the way, you learn more, observe more, connect more, and *do* more, which helps you *serve* more, as a leader.

A simple act of service changes the game. It turns the tide and creates a sense of meaning and purpose in an otherwise mundane job or situation. The bonus is you'll have taken another step in leading with hospitality, making them feel welcome in their role and on your team.

Put *Hospitality in Action*— Activating Service

1. **Listen to your intuition, your team, your leaders, and especially your customers.** When leaders take time to listen, everyone will be well served.

2. **Educate people along the way.** Take the time to pause and teach, coach, and offer feedback, especially recognition. When leaders take advantage of teachable moments today, they pass along nuggets and pearls of wisdom that serve people for a lifetime.

3. **Act.** Live out the concept of *active accountability*, which is simply taking personal accountability and responsibility for staying active and accountable to your team's needs. When

you're active and accountable, your team will be active and accountable.

4. **Deliver on your promise as a leader.** Deliver the information, tools, support, and resources your team needs to perform at their best. When you deliver for your team, they will deliver for your customers.

Action Plan to Lead with Hospitality:

SERVE

Serve your team to help them grow.

We have now reached the end of Part Two—SERVE. Here are this section's prompts and exercises to start leading with hospitality. If you like, you can write in this book. Or grab that notebook or fire up your computer and open up a document. Let's continue!

Be empathetic and always seek to understand how others think and feel about certain situations. Share your understanding and modify your approach, message, and timing of communication accordingly.

List one person on your team whom you believe is struggling in some way. List how you think they're feeling and why. Detail how you'll modify your approach and message to meet them where they are, empathizing with their situation. Have you ever had a similar experience? How might you show them you understand?

_____

_____

_____

_____

_____

_____

Master four fundamentals to LEAD with a servant heart: *Listen, Educate, Act,* **and** *Deliver.*

Listen.

Listen to your intuition. Listen to your team. Listen to your leaders. Listen to your customers.

   List three things you've heard from your **team or your teammates** *that could be worth exploring deeper.*

1. _____

2. _____

3. _____

List three things you've heard from **your own leaders** *that could be opportunities to explore deeper, to improve your team's performance.*

1. _____

2. _____

3. _____

List three things you've heard from **your customers** *that could be worth exploring to improve the experience or service you provide.*

1. _____

2. _____

3. _____

*List three things your **intuition** is telling you right now:*

1. Where do you need to focus more time?

_____

_____

2. What do you need to do for yourself or your team?

_____

_____

3. What might you need to change about your approach?

_____

_____

Educate

Educate your team. Seek out teachable moments and coachable behaviors to serve your team with useful lessons you've learned that you can pass along to them.

Who is one team member who would benefit from some education or a lesson you've observed he or she may need to help them grow? Identify the person, the lesson, and a date and time you'll deliver the lesson.

_____

_____

_____

_____

_____

Act

Take action. Be active by staying aware of your team's progress on their own action plans, inspect what you expect, and have tough conversations on the spot when necessary.

List one area where you know you need to spend more time in the operation, in the areas with your team to become more aware of progress, roadblocks, and opportunities to recognize high performers.

_____

_____

_____

_____

Deliver

Deliver feedback, deliver on your promises, and deliver information, tools, and support to your team on a consistent basis.

Who needs feedback?

Who may need additional information, tools, and support?

Who would benefit from better understanding the promises you have and continue to make to your team as well as how you've delivered on them?

_____

_____

_____

_____

_____

_____

PART THREE

ENGAGE

Chapter 5

COMFORT

*Curiosity, Conversations,
and Relationships Happen
Where People Feel Secure*

*A deep sense of love and belonging is an irreducible need of all
people. We are biologically, cognitively, physically, and spiri-
tually wired to love, to be loved, and to belong. When those
needs are not met, we don't function as we were meant to. We
break. We fall apart. We numb. We ache. We hurt others. We
get sick.*

—Brené Brown

A Washington-based tech giant had a CEO who had a way of
making everyone uncomfortable. He put employees on edge
with his mere presence. He was brilliant, and the company

certainly grew under his leadership, but after a prolonged plateau in performance, the long-term trajectory didn't look good.

He demanded people be know-it-alls, which made them feel awkward and uneasy. Several years ago, this CEO left the business to pursue new opportunities. A new CEO who started as a humble engineer twenty-two years prior was named in February 2014 to fill his shoes.

The new CEO felt the company had lost some of its soul and innovativeness under the previous CEO, with all the edginess and drama. How could he get people excited about coming to work each day again and participating at the highest levels?

Earlier in his career, a very successful man had told him, "You'll probably spend more time working over the years than you'll spend with your kids. For that reason, it's vitally important you do something you believe in and that provides a purpose or meaning to your life."

The advice caused him to truly question and ponder what brought him purpose, meaning, and joy in his work. So when he became a CEO years later, he knew creating a foundation and purpose that aligned the corporation as a whole would make employees feel more comfortable and inspire them to give their best.

He started by first listening intently and getting to know people all over the company. A tall order, as the company has over one hundred thousand employees. He walked into areas and traveled to locations he'd never visited before. He asked questions and took a genuine, caring interest in what people had to say. People liked his fresh, new approach and the fact that he obviously cared about the company and about them as people. They quickly started to calm down and feel more comfortable. This meant they started opening up, talking with each other, and sharing ideas more often.

Then he told everyone, "I don't want you to try to be a know-it-all. I want you to do your best to be a learn-it-all." He wanted them to know what mattered under his leadership was curiosity, asking questions, innovation, and getting comfortable being uncomfortable.

He insisted employees should always feel empowered to push back. In a November 2019 *Fast Company* article, he said, "We pay deep attention to where they're coming from, what's causing their concern, because I think that's super important."[17]

Just three months after he took over, the company's stock price had increased by an impressive 12 percent. Now, over five years into his much more comfortable leadership and learn-it-all culture, the company's stock price has tripled.

That company is Microsoft.

Since Satya Nadella started as the CEO of Microsoft, he's guided the company through what experts refer to as "a renaissance." Microsoft has experienced several outstanding years in terms of revenues and profits, even topping Amazon's revenues during some months. They also rank high in comfortable employees who aren't afraid to learn and speak up rather than try to be know-it-alls. He's done it by being a human leader, listening and being humble, rather than trying to be a superhuman one.

Make Them Feel Comfortable

Making people feel comfortable is the second transferable thread between hospitality and leadership. In the Microsoft story and countless others, great things can happen when people feel comfortable. When people feel comfortable, they

- open up and engage in more conversations;
- feed their curiosity with more exploration, research, and discovery;

+ foster deeper relationships with people around them; and
+ feel a sense of belonging in the workplace.

Consider the reverse for a moment. When people feel *un*comfortable in a situation or around certain people, they

+ don't want to talk to anyone and keep to themselves;
+ have very little curiosity to learn anything new;
+ foster few meaningful relationships in that uncomfortable space; and
+ absolutely, positively don't feel like they belong or fit in.

How does your team feel right now?

Better yet, how do you want your team to feel? I've explained the two alternatives—either comfortable or uncomfortable—in polarizing extremes. But give this some thought. How does your team feel today? Maybe more importantly, how do you need your team to feel?

Leadership is about inspiring and influencing the absolute best effort and the best versions of everyone on the team. Therefore, it behooves any leader in any industry at any level to make their team feel comfortable enough to be their best, give their best, and become the absolute best they can be.

> According to the American Institute of Stress, 83 percent of US workers suffer from work-related stress.[18]
>
> In another survey by Korn Ferry, 35 percent of respondents said their main source of stress at work was their boss.[19]

Conversations and Collaboration

When your team feels comfortable, they'll lean into being the most productive versions of themselves. This is at the forefront of our leadership purpose, to encourage everyone to perform up to their maximum potential.

Conversations are like magic super fuel that drives engines of culture, connection, and collaboration. They ignite people who propel organizations. Companies and even divisions of companies can have the best products in the world, the smartest strategies, and the most dialed-in tactical game plan, but without a great culture, strong connections, and thriving collaboration, any success will be short lived. The responsibility of leadership is to engage each member of the team in conversation and to ignite conversations among team members.

Change is hard for everyone because, with change, we're pushed outside our comfort zones. With each step further and further outside our comfort zones, we often have more questions than we have answers. The fear of the unknown can keep people trapped inside their comfort zone, which sadly can keep people and organizations from experiencing new realms of success, happiness, and accomplishment.

Brainstorming, trying new things, and expressing opinions can make us all feel very vulnerable! As leaders, our role is to help people get more comfortable being uncomfortable in these types of conversations. All we have to do is make sure teams feel comfortable and safe to try new things that might not work. In chapter 4, I mentioned that The Cosmopolitan of Las Vegas was my favorite career stop. It was exciting and meaningful for many reasons, but perhaps the single-best thing about our culture was that *trying new things* wasn't just a suggestion. It was the expectation.

We were encouraged to be different and just try it if and when we had an idea. As long as we learned from our experiments and trial runs and communicated those learnings, everyone was okay with it. That sentiment alone made vulnerability cool and worth venturing into as opposed to shying away from it.

Curiosity

Eric Schmidt, CEO of Google from 2001 to 2017, once said, "We run this company on questions, not answers."[20] Most people would agree this is a powerful approach and mindset for any company or leader to possess. By the way, Schmidt is personally worth about $12 billion today.[21] Need I say more?

Sure, a wildly successful company like Google may be an obvious example, but the principle remains. Without curiosity, organizations seldom innovate, and without innovation, organizations are dead in the water. Leading with hospitality is the proven way to make sure our teams know it's okay to challenge, ask *why* or *why not*, and most importantly, take time to study, learn, and develop. Make sure your teams stay curious, because curiosity will help them stay relevant, stay ahead, and stay hungry. An atmosphere and culture of curiosity starts at the top with you, the leader of your team. Leadership is awesome. As in, it can be awe-inspiring, to positively impact and change the lives of the people you lead.

When it comes to creating curious teams, you have two choices:

You can be a know-it-all and have a my-way-or-the-highway approach, which won't inspire much organic curiosity or questioning.

Or you can be honest about sharing what you don't know and what you'd like to learn. The latter approach requires being secure enough in your own skin to unleash your capable, talented, and spirited team's curiosity. When you do, they will feel free and comfortable about helping in areas where you may lack knowledge or ideas.

I'd rather lead with hospitality and allow my team to have a voice, an identity, and give them full permission to be curious, where innovation can take root and grow. You'll want and need your teams to ask the right questions at the right times of the right people, consistently peeling the onion back, exploring and discovering new ways to do business. As leaders, you rely on your teams for feedback, keeping your eyes and ears open on the front lines. They're in the thick of it, every hour of every day. They see, feel, think, and do things you don't always have the opportunity to experience.

Suggestions for process improvements can come from no better place than from your teams. They know what works and what doesn't work. Imagine the sense of purpose and enjoyment you'll create with team members when you encourage them to be curious, try new things, and express their never-ending thirst for knowledge. Create that purpose, curiosity, and sense of enjoyment by making sure they're comfortable.

Relationships

One of my past leaders always quoted one of his former leaders. He'd say, "There are results, and there are reasons. And the reasons don't matter."

Perhaps you're scratching your head. I loved, respected, and appreciated this leader. However, this one sentiment of his always left me feeling uneasy and annoyed. I get the whole deliver-results message. After all, that's ultimately why people are hired for any job. For entrepreneurs, results are one of the most important objectives. Without them, well, it's just an expensive hobby.

However, those who genuinely lead with hospitality realize while results are important, fostering meaningful relationships is a critically important first step in bringing the desired results to fruition. Whether in sports or individual contributor roles in corporate America, entire teams of people must come together and form symbiotic relationships with one another to achieve desired results.

For example, tennis great Serena Williams didn't become Serena overnight. She had and still has teams of people helping her prepare and perform at her best, on and off the tennis court. Same with Tiger Woods, as he's on swing coach number five or six.

Salespeople can be influential, gain trust, and ultimately sign up new business. But without the support of quality assurance teams, finance teams, marketing teams, and even operations teams on the front lines, they'd soon be up a creek without a paddle, unable to drive tangible results over the long haul.

In hotels, interdepartmental relationships between housekeeping and front desk, finance and marketing, and even sales and operations must be rock solid for the overarching, collective hotel team to be successful at driving results. In schools, teachers, librarians, administrators, teacher's assistants, and the superintendent's office must be in sync to educate young minds and prepare them for achievement tests, not to mention a successful academic and professional career.

The same is true for any business, group, or organization. You can harp, micromanage, grandstand in meetings, and point fingers all day long, but until you step up and genuinely foster real relationships and a relationship-centric culture, your desired results will be few and far between. Even if some results happen, they won't last over the long haul.

So much of this is what we were never taught in high school, college, or even graduate school. Relationship-ing in business and life is like rebounding in basketball. You just have to want it. You must wake up every day with a mindset and desire for connection with people. The cool part about sparking relationships is it usually costs no money. The only investments needed are time and genuine interest.

Leading with hospitality means actively spending time with one's team, partners, peers, mentors, and especially guests, customers, and clients. That's step one, but step two is the most important and possibly the most *hospitable* step. That is, to take an interest in people.

Nothing turns people off more than a boss who pontificates, spits, and spews on and on about how awesome they are, how much they know, how much they make, or how perfect they were when they were in your role. Remember the superhuman leader from chapter 3, the one who holds all six Infinity Stones? If there were such things as "Leadership Standings," they would lead the league in "The Worst Conversations Ever," not to mention coming in dead last in the "Quantity of Relationships Made" category.

Conversely, nothing makes people feel more comfortable and ready to deliver results more than thriving, productive, and meaningful relationships at work. There is one additional thing. In fact, it's not a thing. He or she is a person, someone who leads with hospitality.

Maybe you've experienced this type of leader, or maybe you've experienced the opposite. Either way, you have an innate desire and need for human connection in your life, which includes the need to foster relationships with and among your team where you work. Since those people you're leading at work are also human, they have those same needs for connection and genuine relationships. Lean into it and watch your team become comfortable with you and their surroundings, and shortly thereafter, you'll see and feel the impact of their brilliance in your organization's results.

It all starts with relationships.

Belonging

Finally, when your team feels comfortable, they begin to feel like they belong. When people feel like they belong, even the drabbest, most mundane job is transformed into meaningful work. This is often the difference between a thriving, accepting corporate culture and a demoralizing one. Frequently, culture within an organization can be the secret sauce that drives results, propelling companies ahead of their competition. Cultures where people feel a sense of belonging attract more like-minded talented employees to the organization as well as like-minded customers. Often, the story of an organization's passionate culture creates emotional connections with guests, customers, and clients. Starbucks, Zappos, Hilton Hotels, Kimpton Hotels, and Disney Parks and Resorts are all examples of organizations that attract customers *and* talented employees as a result of their culture.

The same will be true for your team when you create a sense of belonging where they work.

If you conscientiously follow the steps below, you'll notice people putting in more effort, giving their best, and coming to work excited each day.

 Put *Hospitality in Action*— Activating Comfort

1. **Make sure people feel comfortable coming to work.** Build community. Few leaders and even fewer organizations activate a true sense of community all of us are literally wired to crave. Relationships will ultimately expedite your results. Be human and be vulnerable enough to connect on a human level, and then just watch your team soar.

2. **Make sure people feel comfortable asking questions.** Be curious and give your team permission to be even more curious. Foster a never-ending thirst for knowledge, intel, insight,

feedback, and opportunities for your organization to grow. Today's best practices may not be enough to sustain or propel your team forward tomorrow. A comfortable culture of curiosity and openness keeps everyone engaged and keeps you competitive.

3. **Help people get comfortable getting uncomfortable.** Your role, as a leader, whether at home, in your community, or at work, is to help people become the best versions of themselves. That means your *leadership purpose* is to help people grow by stepping outside their comfort zones. The only way people grow, improve, and truly *become* better is to step outside their comfort zones. When you realize the task, the job, the situation, or even the season is becoming more difficult, you begin to discover just how good, capable, committed, and talented you are. Your team will experience the same.

People want to improve, but they need an encourager, a champion, and leader to give them a nudge. That's you.

Chapter 6

GENUINE KINDNESS

A Gift Worth Giving because
It's Always Well Received

To the world you may be one person, but to one person you may
be the world.

—Dr. Seuss

A t first, I was going to title this chapter "Courtesy." I'm a big fan of courtesy. It's so *genteel* and all. Then I realized, a person can be courteous—considerate, well behaved, polite, and well mannered—always saying the right things at the right time to the right people. But unless courtesy comes from a place of genuine consideration for others, it's an empty, meaningless gesture. Given enough time, most people begin to see right through a phony front of forced courtesy.

While being considerate and acting with common courtesy are certainly value-added traits, leading with hospitality moves people to act with purpose and passion because of a leader's genuine kindness. In other words, when leaders are real and authentic as opposed to putting up a front, trying to portray a certain image or persona for their own self-serving reasons, their teams become far more comfortable in their roles. When teams feel comfortable in their roles, we're well on our way to creating an environment suitable for them to crush it. This is the point of leadership, which is to inspire and influence people to give their very best effort toward a specific, collective cause or goal.

In *Harvard Business Review*'s "Discovering Your Authentic Leadership," Bill George, Peter Sims, Andrew N. McLean, and Diana Mayer presented an exploration of the styles, characteristics, and personality traits of leaders.[22] I love this quote from their article:

"No one can be authentic by trying to imitate someone else. You can learn from others' experiences, but there is no way you can be successful when you are trying to be like them. People trust you when you are genuine and authentic."

I've always believed leadership is like sales, and sales is a form of leadership. Why? For a leader to be successful at leading anyone toward anything, and for a salesperson to be successful in selling anyone anything, they must both earn the trust of another person. One of the quickest ways to earn trust from people is to simply be trustworthy, honest, and open. A genuinely kind person is certainly worthy of being trusted far more than someone who always "fakes it until they make it."

Kindness Is Truly a Gift

Webster's Dictionary defines *kindness* as "the quality of being friendly, generous, and considerate." Call me a nerd, but let's take it a step farther and also check the definition of *generous*: "showing a readiness to give more of something than is strictly necessary or expected."

The beauty and underlying massive opportunity to display genuine kindness in leadership is that it's often so unexpected. The day-to-day doldrums of our jobs, the expectations and standards, the pressure, and the constant need to impress can clog up our minds. That makes it incredibly more impactful when people receive our genuine kindness. They're just not used to it.

While that's sad, it's also proof we need more leaders who lead with hospitality. Because it's a huge opportunity to *give* of ourselves to our teams. When leaders show up with kindness and genuine concern for their teams as humans and individuals, the results are amazing. Make a shift in mindset to generously *give* of yourself. Giving isn't always noticed, nor is it always acknowledged, but trust me: it's always well received.

For example, have you ever heard someone say, "Boy, I sure wish he or she would stop being so kind all the time"? Me neither. Our genuine kindness has the potential to inspire, help, encourage, teach, coach, improve, and enhance the work of others and their lives. That's reason enough to give kindness.

What about the people who receive your kindness and concern with doubt or suspicion? Perhaps they left a job where the culture was toxic. Or maybe in their personal life kindness always came with strings attached. Keep at it. Over time, your genuine kindness and interest will eventually touch them personally, which will lead to new realms of engagement and execution professionally.

GiVE

GiVE Culture is a California-based lifestyle brand that sells T-shirts, hats, sweatshirts, and other merch that simply have "GiVE _____" prominently placed across the front. Their products have printed statements like:

- GiVE Encouragement
- GiVE Thanks
- GiVE Hope
- GiVE Compassion
- GiVE Love
- GiVE Patience
- GiVE Peace
- GiVE Praise
- GiVE Hospitality
- GiVE Kindness

The *i* is purposely lowercased, because to truly *give* anything means to put others first, ahead of our own agendas.

I first met GiVE Culture and their products at a food-and-wine festival in Orange County, California. I met the founding partners of the brand, Noel and Shauna Felix, who told me their story. They were both former athletes at Fresno State University and Christian people simply creating something to hold individuals (and themselves) accountable for their actions toward others.

Together, they've set out to "shine a little light on love." Their website describes the company as "A socially conscious lifestyle brand designed to inspire and encourage mindfulness and generosity in an increasingly divided world."[23]

I immediately fell in love with them, their brand, and their cause. I bought three shirts, GiVE Compassion, GiVE Encouragement, and GiVE Kindness right on the spot. Their genuine compassion, encouragement, and outright love for people inspired me, and I wanted to be like them. I wanted in, as a part of their cause. I proudly wear my GiVE T-shirts around town, when I travel, and even when I speak to audiences on leadership, teamwork, and personal growth.

You may be wondering how a lovey-dovey T-shirt brand pertains to leading with hospitality. I was compelled to tell you about GiVE Culture and the brand because it's a beautiful blueprint and an illustration of genuine kindness. They believe that wearing the shirt can be a consistent reminder to shift your mindset and put others first. Through their GiVE Culture Foundation for Impact, they create live learning experiences at schools, camps, and conferences. Their lessons—for teachers *and* for kids—inspire and encourage a spirit of mindfulness, selflessness, and generosity among the next generation of students and leaders all across the Unites States. As a leader in business and life, you can create, inspire, and scale a "GiVE Culture" in your teams and organizations by simply *being* the change you want to see around you.

A study found that teams in a respectful environment:[24]

- Possess 26 percent more energy.
- Are 30 percent more likely to feel motivated and enthusiastic about acquiring new skills and being exposed to new ideas.
- Express 36 percent more satisfaction with their jobs and are 44 percent more committed to their organizations.

Kindness Is Contagious

Just as I was inspired by my new friends at GiVE Culture because of their genuineness, your teams will be inspired by your genuine kindness, as you lead with hospitality. The old leadership adage "Model the behaviors you want to see" fits perfectly here. Kindness truly is a choice, and, when leaders actively choose to be kind to the people they lead, those people will naturally follow. They'll want in.

If they see and hear you seeking to understand before seeking to be understood, they'll follow your lead. When they catch a glimpse of you being genuinely interested in how you can help them, their peers, and even your guests, customers, and clients, they'll take a genuine interest in doing the same. Even when they see a simple gesture like you opening a door for someone or letting others go first at the coffee machine, they will get the message. And because kindness is contagious, as they watch how you listen intently and empathetically to other team members, they'll begin emulating those actions, sentiments, and genuine kindness with each other; and most importantly, with your customers.

Kindness Is Inspiring

I love the quote "Be kind, for everyone you meet is fighting a hard battle you know nothing about." The same goes for every person on your team. As I mentioned earlier, the one thing every person has in common with one another is we're all human beings. People are people. Therefore, every person is experiencing real people problems. (Except, of course, the superhuman leader who has no flaws or problems. They're practically perfect in every way, like Mary Poppins.)

As mentioned earlier, when your team slowly but surely realizes you're there to help them, not hold them back, the tide changes. As time goes on, when people see you walk the talk, giving your own time, talents, and gifts to others, they're inspired to do the same.

Those gifts can be tangible ones as well as intangible ones. Here are just a few examples where an act of leadership kindness can uplift your team:

- Give a genuine compliment, recognizing their efforts.
- Provide sincere feedback to help them become even more successful.
- Give them the afternoon off when you know they've been overdoing it.
- Something as simple as a thank-you can inspire greater action, purpose, meaning, and passion in their work.
- Just a quick high-five while walking down the hallway may lift their spirits at just the right time when they need it the most.
- Or simply listen to them when they need it.

Show me a genuinely kind leader, and I'll show you someone who can successfully ignite action, meaningful work, and passion in and among a team. Passionate teams who engage in meaningful work deliver consistent results. Their results speak for themselves. Everyone who works there will say they work as hard as they do because of the welcoming, comfortable culture of their beloved organization.

Put *Hospitality in Action*— Activating Kindness

1. **Give your time.** Set aside time for each person on your team. Plan for it and give some time for the benefit of others. It will be noticed, appreciated, and worth it for both you and for them. Take thirty minutes each day to focus on one person on your team. Explore what you can do to help them, either personally or professionally. Pick a different person each day for a week or a month or more until you've made it through your entire roster of team members. Then go back to the beginning of the list and repeat.

2. **Give your talent.** Whatever is your greatest strength, your best talent, and "that awesome thing" people say you do better than anyone else, zero in on it and flat out give it away to people. I'm not saying work for free. I'm simply recommending to freely *give* of yourself to others, especially your natural strengths and talent. You're gifted in some way. To be a great leader, *give your gifts* to those you lead, and you'll soon see them do the same to your guests, customers, clients, and especially to their team-mates. That's the essence of creating a GiVE Culture where you work. Giving the best of yourself while looking for and bringing out the best in others.

3. **Give your heart.** Perhaps the kindest, most welcomed, and most comforting thing about any human being is when we know they care. When you give your heart to people on your team, you'll inspire them to perform at their best and give more of what makes them great as well. Kindness is contagious. It's worth spreading at work, at home, and in our communities.

Chapter 7

ENCOURAGEMENT
Uplifting People Fuels Hearts, Which Fuels Minds, Which Fuels Successful Teams

Be an encourager. The world has enough critics already.
—Unknown

In the early 1980s, a girl named Emily was born in Roehampton, South West London, England. She was very smart, active, and a great student, but throughout grade school and junior high, she had a stammering stutter. It was so debilitating, it caused her to shy away from engaging in conversation with people. She had so much she wanted to say; but she couldn't say it. Her issue haunted her much of her childhood and adolescence.

When Emily was in junior high school, one of her teachers encouraged her to try out for a school play. He thought she would be great in a role where she'd have to speak with an accent. Emily was mortified at the mere possibility, but her teacher encouraged her to give it a try. He'd given it great thought and truly believed she'd perform the part beautifully. He also felt confident speaking with an accent would help Emily get over her stutter.

With the backing of her teacher, Emily took the next step. She got the role, starred in the play, and in the process, found herself so immersed in her character with the accent, her stuttering disappeared. Her teacher was right. She probably would never have taken the step to audition if not for her teacher's support.

Emily went on to star in plays and television dramas in Great Britain. You may know her from her breakout film role in *The Devil Wears Prada*, when she played Emily, the annoying, rude, and obnoxious assistant to Meryl Streep's character, Miranda, opposite Anne Hathaway's performance as Andy.

Young Emily with a stuttering problem as a child grew to become Emily Blunt. Yes, that Emily Blunt. The successful actress and performer who's won a Golden Globe and starred in movies including *The Devil Wears Prada*, *The Young Victoria*, *Edge of Tomorrow*, *The Girl on the Train*, *A Quiet Place*, and *Mary Poppins Returns*, as Mary Poppins. As an adult, she's starred in over thirty movies between 2000 and 2020 (at the time of this writing), more than ten roles on television, and four roles in live stage productions.

Emily's teacher saw something in her, believed in her, and encouraged her.[25] That's what leaders who lead with hospitality do. They encourage. When people like young Emily Blunt lack confidence, hope, and even support, leaders like her teacher back in South West London, England instill all three—confidence, hope, and support.

As we wrap up our conversation on making our teams feel comfortable, this chapter explores the power of encouragement. It has been, is, and will continue to be one of the biggest drivers in your ability to help people on your teams feel comfortable in their own skin, in their role, and on your team. Making them feel engaged with your encouragement will ignite levels of productivity you never thought possible.

There are many ways to deliver encouragement to our teams, as leaders who lead with hospitality. If you don't know how to encourage people on your teams, keep reading. I'm confident when you implement the following ideas that it will make a world of difference. People will stand a little taller. They'll participate more and step up their game to give you their best. For some, the change will be instant. Others will take a little more time. Stay the course and watch the difference unfold.

I've chosen three simple, actionable ways for leaders to encourage people. The purpose is to make your teams feel more comfortable and confident in their abilities to step up, lean in, and deliver their best work. As a leader, you can encourage through *recognition, reminders,* and *assistance.*

Recognition: Sawubona Means "We See You"

The Zulu people make up the largest ethnic group in South Africa. As with any tribe, their culture is deeply rooted in their history and heritage. In Zulu culture, which has influenced the South African culture, there's a familiar and simple greeting, "Sawubona."

Sawubona literally means, "We see you."

The response, "Yebo sawubona," means, "Yes, we see you too."[26]

Going a bit deeper, these two words carry a much more profound meaning, which I originally read about in a few articles.[27] The more I read and learned about it, the more I wanted to gain a greater understanding. As I came to understand the profound values in this culture, the more inspired I felt. In fact, organizations from small businesses to large corporations would be well served to follow the Zulu's lead.

Inherent in the Zulu greeting, "Sawubona," and the reply, "Yebo sawubona," is a sense that we see each other. It's more than a greeting and even more than an interaction. It's a way of life and a way of being that says because we see each other, we can really begin to explore our collective potential, together.

In Transition

Have you ever been unemployed, or as we currently refer to it, "in transition"? It's zero fun. Well, it's kind of cool the first few weeks. You go to the pool, sleep in, binge on Netflix, and enjoy time off. Then, after another few weeks of job applications, cover letters, and scouring the web looking for your "next chapter," reality sets in.

Maybe you've also been in transition. If you have, you know how it feels to mope around at home, at the grocery store, or at the gym. The few times you go out with friends or family, it almost feels like you're less of a human. In that chapter of your life, it is very difficult to feel *encouraged* or *engaged*.

You look around at other people and see them with their jobs for which they earn paychecks. With their paycheck they buy groceries, cocktails, tacos, and gifts for families and friends. You wonder, "Will I ever know what it's like to see a paycheck deposited in my account again?"

Once when I was "in transition," I'd applied for nearly two hundred jobs for which I wasn't even granted an interview. In fact, nobody even acknowledged my existence. I could have used a little *sawubona* in my life.

Until one day, I received a message from a company to which I had applied. Instantly, I felt alive again. It was like someone flipped a switch.

Before, I was moping through the grocery store with few positive thoughts. Now someone was interested! Someone recognized my years of experience, maybe it was my blog, my picture on LinkedIn, or perhaps my resume. Thank goodness, someone recognized my potential.

Suddenly, I felt like I existed on Earth, like maybe I could add the value I knew deep down I was capable of contributing. In a moment, I walked taller, with more purpose. I felt more confident in my abilities and capabilities. I was encouraged because someone recognized me.

When you finally get the job, or even when you've been in a job for several years, you're still human. You still have feelings, doubts, stresses, worries, and anxieties. When you're a leader of people, starring in the real-life television drama that is your career, it's easy to lose sight of your humanness. Emails don't stop. Meetings and conference calls keep popping up on your calendar. Results, objectives, deadlines, and deliverables hang over your head like pesky gnats in the summertime trying to ruin your watermelon. (Although nothing can ever really *ruin* watermelon.)

At Least They See Me

In busy seasons like this, as a leader, it's easy to forget the work you're responsible for is performed and carried out by human beings. They're human just like you. Remember: while I was "in transition," with an absence of recognition, I felt less human and incapable, not to mention wildly uncomfortable. The people on our teams might also feel discouraged and uncomfortable when their work is unrecognized. What's worse is when people trudge to and from work every day, yet they remain unnoticed and unknown to their leaders.

People want to be noticed and known. Leaders who lead with hospitality make it a point, their duty, and even their way of life to recognize people. We should all embody the culture of the Zulu people, and make sure people know we see them. Especially if you're a leader tasked with delivering results—financial results, productivity results, output results, service score results, and so on. You'll have a head start toward those results when you lead with hospitality. When you recognize people for the work they do and for the people they are, they can't help but feel encouraged.

Once people feel encouraged, they'll take a deep breath and let out a huge sigh of relief that almost says, "Well, at least they see me and my contributions." Voila! You've taken a giant leap in making them feel engaged. This becomes the first spark that ignites creativity, commitment, and passion in their work, not to mention the courage to step up and lean into giving their best so the team delivers those results you have in mind. After all, to encourage is to literally *give someone courage.*

Like a great door person, valet, or bell person in a hotel *recognizes* a valued guest by using the guest's name, offering to carry the guest's luggage when they notice the guest had a long day of travel, park the guest's car when it's raining, or even turn on a space heater when they notice the guest is shivering on the front drive, leaders who lead with hospitality recognize the needs of valued people on their teams.

> According to a survey, 82 percent of employed Americans don't feel their supervisors recognize them enough for their contributions.[28]

How can you recognize the people on your teams so they will be more engaged?

Once a former boss sent me a text while I was on vacation, letting me know our employee satisfaction survey results were tallied. The team we oversaw rated their leaders (my boss and me), their experience, and overall job satisfaction as extremely high. We received some of the highest scores in the organization.

My boss's text was short and simple. It read, "Your team's scores were some of the highest in the company, and I'm honored to work with you. Thanks for doing what you do." Simple, yet one of the most encouraging messages I've ever received. The most encouraging thing was she recognized my efforts.

Recognize people on your teams and let them know how much you see and appreciate what they're doing for you, the team, and your customers.

Sawubona.

Reminders

"People need to be reminded more often than they need to be instructed." This famous quote comes from Samuel Johnson, an English author, critic, and lexicographer (yeah, he literally *compiled* dictionaries) in the 1700s.[29]

I love this quote because it's a great way to lead. In fact, it's a great way to lead with hospitality, especially when creating a comfortable setting for people on our teams. Consider which is more encouraging: a boss pontificating, instructing you on every move, how to do this and how not to do that, or an engaging leader who, in moments of doubt or discomfort, offers reminders of what you've accomplished, the opportunities ahead of you, or the potential you have within to create something amazing?

Leaders who lead with hospitality constantly remind people of what they've accomplished to encourage them for the work that lies ahead. Nobody is perfect, and very seldom is anyone good enough to achieve perfection at the inception of a project or new initiative. Often, it takes practice and repetition after repetition. However, most people have accomplishments in their past that have shaped them as people and put them on the road to their present circumstances. They've made progress.

A great leader who leads with hospitality reminds people where they've been, the roads they've traveled, the hills they've climbed, and the adversities they've overcome. I'll take this moment to remind you that you've also overcome obstacles in your past. While you haven't been perfect, you've made progress. People on your team need to hear the same message, and you're the person to deliver it.

It takes little heart or soul to point out precise instructions or the how-tos for a task or assignment. It takes only a minute or two to point out, instruct, and direct. We see it often. Leaders doing drive by management.

Or as bestselling author Ken Blanchard calls it, "seagull leadership"—when leaders fly in, drop a bunch of stuff, and fly back to their pedestals.[30]

Sure, the message is communicated. Leaders who lack depth, substance, and soul, not to mention hospitality, feel better after unloading the message. Yet they wonder why their messages never really land and rarely compel people or teams to act.

(Or at least perform the action that matters most.)

At one point, I had recently transitioned from a role in hotel operations to become a leader in sales and marketing for Walt Disney Parks and Resorts. It was around the holidays, and a former colleague in operations invited me as her guest to the holiday party where I worked prior to my transition. I was about three months into my new role in sales and marketing, and still uncomfortable. It was all new, and I was deep in learning mode.

At the party, I ran into my former general manager of the resort from which I'd recently transferred. His name was Dave Vermeulen, whose career started by selling popcorn on Main Street USA at Disneyland in 1965 (just ten years after Walt opened the doors in 1955). During the next forty-eight years, he went on to lead teams in Disney theme parks and resorts, slowly but surely moving up along the way.

He asked me how things were going in my new position. He was as interested in me as ever, though I no longer worked in his organization. I told him I was a bit uneasy still. It was a whole new world (no pun intended).

He looked me in the eye, put his hand on my shoulder, and simply reminded me of all I'd accomplished up to that point. He reminded me, while I'd never worked in sales or marketing before, I'd led teams of people in multiple lines of business in hotel operations. He reminded me the same skills, talents, and abilities that enabled me to perform as a leader earlier in my career would also be used in my new role. Sure, it was a simple message, but I'll never forget how encouraged I felt that evening, especially when I felt so uncomfortable in my new role.

I recall rolling into work the following Monday morning with a brand-new mindset and newfound confidence. After being reminded of my accomplishments, capabilities, and potential, I was ready to set the world on fire again.

I've kept tabs on Dave's career since those days back in the early 2000s. It's no surprise Disney tapped him to lead the entire resort operations line of business for the opening of Hong Kong Disneyland for three years. To close out his career, he was vice president and executive managing director of Walt Disney Attractions—Japan. Even since his retirement in 2013, Disney still requests Dave's leadership on a contract basis as he supports Disney Parks & Resorts Asia in an emeritus role.

Clearly *encouraging* people, leading with hospitality over a lifetime of varying roles, got him noticed and selected. I'm glad I was lucky enough to be an up-and-comer to whom Dave gave his heart and soul. He changed my way of thinking, believing, and leading the rest of my career with his simple, heartfelt words. Now I'm inspired to reassure others to do the same, and I know you are too.

Assistance: Be Like Joe

Have you ever worked at a less than glamourous job? Most of us have probably been blessed with a not-so-sexy gig at one point or another. What often turns a less than glamourous or seemingly meaningless job into a meaningful one is dynamic leadership. I experienced some very dynamic leadership on a summer internship at Disney's All-Star Movies Resort back in June of 2000.

We'd made it through Y2K successfully. However, during the summer of 2000, I was working the 5:00 PM to 1:30 AM shift at Donald's Double Feature, one of the highest revenue-producing merchandise locations in the entire forty-eight-square miles of the vacation kingdom, the Walt Disney World Resort in beautiful (humid) Orlando, Florida.

A couple summers prior, I'd worked in quick-service food and beverage at Hurricane Hannah's Bar & Grill, at Disney's Yacht and Beach Club Resort. In that role, every time I ran the register up front, my cash drawer never balanced at the end of the night: wrong change, taking in too much money inadvertently, dropping and fumbling coins behind the register. You name it, I did it, usually incorrectly. I was so bad at keeping up the pace at the cash register that, three weeks into the program, I had asked to switch from front to back of house to flip burgers and prepare sandwiches, salads, and PB&Js in back for the remaining two months of the internship.

At least in back, I couldn't possibly mess up the money part, and I could crank country music on a radio in the kitchen, put my head down, and pump out orders. Thankfully for me (and all the guests at Disney's Yacht and Beach Club's pool between June and August 1998), my request to be relieved of my cash register duty was granted.

Fast-forward two summers, and here I was again, faced with another opportunity to create magic for guests with my exemplary cash-handling skills, at a merchandise location (that's "Disney-ese" for a resort gift shop) with tens of thousands of transactions every week. The resort had just under two thousand rooms, and the shop was also located adjacent to a local bus stop. Every ten to fifteen minutes that summer, it was like a rock concert let out into our store. Predictably, I was a nervous wreck at the thought of dealing with so many transactions.

Then I met Joe, one of my managers.

Joe was personable, relatable, and as genuine as anyone I'd ever met, let alone any boss I'd had up to that point in my illustrious "internship career." On any given shift or day, you'd almost always find Joe out on the floor with his cast and guests. Usually, he was holding an armful of products on his way to stock a shelf or a revolving fixture of trading pins.

He was constantly helping. What I always noticed, and thought was outstanding, was that while he was out stocking shelves, he was always listening and observing.

He helped guests and cast members. He helped his leaders. Early on that summer, he certainly helped me. I told him about my less than stellar performance at the cash register a couple summers prior. I also told him I'd never really worked retail before. I was nervous and visibly uncomfortable.

He didn't skip a beat. First and foremost, he made me feel comfortable right off the bat by learning as much about me as possible. He was genuinely interested. He asked about my family, where I was from in Kentucky, what my favorite sports were. He asked if I had a girlfriend, what my buddies and I liked to do on our days off, and most importantly, he asked what I wanted to get out of that summer. The more interested he became in me, the more comfortable I felt.

It was encouraging to have a leader focus on me.

I answered his questions while emphasizing what I wanted out of that summer internship. I was graduating from Florida Southern College the following spring. My goal was to return to Walt Disney World as a salaried leader upon college graduation. I told Joe that was what I wanted more than anything. His unforgettable answer made me feel even more comfortable. In fact, his reply inspired me to do the same for anyone and everyone I've led since.

Joe said, "Well, it's my job to help you get there."

Joe had observed me for a couple weeks. He noticed I was outgoing with fellow teammates, and I was obviously passionate about the brand. He could tell I loved Disney. He also noticed I was a bit slow on the cash register. That's where he zeroed in—and he assisted me (see the Put Hospitality in Action—Activating Encouragement box on page 122).

Joe purposely placed me at the busiest cash register in the store. He even modified some of my shifts to align with the busiest hours of the day so I'd get as much practice as possible. He taught me the ins and outs of retail, including the importance of well-stocked shelves, maximizing revenue per square foot, attractive visual displays, and upselling. Early on, he stood by my side at the cash register to help me if I became overwhelmed.

With every shift, I became more comfortable, especially at the register. Since I was forced out of my comfort zone and into nonstop repetition and transactions, the mechanics of working the register became second nature. Then, Joe encouraged me to use my outgoing personality, firsthand knowledge of Disney theme parks and resorts, and passion for hospitality in my interaction with guests.

By the end of the summer, I was picking up extra overtime shifts and training newcomers who were the next round of interns arriving for the fall semester. I grew to love my job.

If someone purchased an autograph book, I'd suggest an oversized character pen to go with it. If they purchased a shirt, I recommended socks to accessorize it. If they purchased a hat, I'd suggest a pin to go on it. Even when people bought something as simple as a bottle of orange juice, I'd recommend vodka to go with it. Joe once overheard my conversation with a customer as he was stocking a nearby shelf one morning. He looked at me and cracked up when the guest said, "Sure. Give me a bottle of Absolut. What the heck!"

All the while, I was operating the cash register efficiently, accurately, and with proficiency, because Joe helped me feel more comfortable. In fact, he'd helped me get comfortable getting uncomfortable. Disney called this *merchantainment*. I loved that little dab of pixie dust and the slight, yet powerful Disney difference.

Sure enough, after graduation from Florida Southern College in the spring of 2001, I was hired as a salaried leader and guest-service manager at Disney's Contemporary Resort for a management internship. Joe's interest, along with his encouragement and assistance the previous summer, inspired me to take a similar approach and leadership style with my new team then and with every team since.

When it comes to helping people feel comfortable, remember that sometimes as leaders, it's our responsibility to help people get comfortable being uncomfortable. That's what Joe did when he positioned me at the busiest register. I was totally out of my comfort zone at first, but it pushed me to learn and grow. The more we help people learn and grow, the harder they'll work to further the team. This always bodes well for optimizing those pesky business results you must deliver as a leader.

If you're unaccustomed to giving recognition, reminders, and assistance, I've compiled some easy steps to activate encouragement below. It's not difficult, but it may require you to get out of your own comfort zone a bit. When you do, the people on your teams will appreciate you for making them feel more comfortable. They will also rise to the occasion, delivering their best more frequently, taking your team further, quicker. You will have inspired it all with good, old-fashioned encouragement.

 ### Put *Hospitality in Action*— Activating Encouragement

1. **Recognize.** Recognize people publicly, privately, on voicemail, in text messages, and even on social media, if the situation presents itself. As with most things in this book, it's less about what you do and more about how you make them feel. With all their contributions, big and small, let them know just how much you appreciate what they're doing for the organization.
   - Recognize effort.
   - Recognize uniqueness.

- Recognize special talents.

   Simple recognition often means the most. Call people by their names or even give them nicknames (positive ones, of course, as long as they're okay with that). This lets them know you "see them" and recognize them as unique individuals, special enough to deserve your interest and attention.

2. **Remind.** Remind people of their successes and the obstacles they've overcome. Playing old tape may not work in some contexts, but it's never a bad move when you genuinely remind people how great they've been in the past. This will reinforce the idea of stepping up and leaning into their greatest potential today and tomorrow.

   - Remind people of their strengths.
   - Remind people of what they've accomplished.
   - Remind people of their potentials, renewing their passion.

3. **Assist.** Whether it's for five minutes, five hours, or five days at a time, take the time to help those on your team. Few leadership actions are as encouraging as leaders of teams out in the field, on the floor, and in the moments that matter as they help their teams. They'll feel it, and you'll feel it in their emotional connection to you and your organization and in their go-the-extra-mile performance.

   - Help people understand their roles and how they fit into the bigger picture.
   - Help people execute their roles by working alongside them.
   - Help people get *comfortable being uncomfortable*, because that's when they'll grow and become the absolute best.

Be like Joe, as I described earlier in this chapter. There's nothing more encouraging than a leader who goes into each day by your side, helping you as opposed to holding power over you. Leading with hospitality is about encouraging and helping. Individuals on your team will feel the difference, and you'll begin to see the impact. Productivity will increase, and shortly thereafter, so will your most desired business results like profitability and sustainability, not to mention a thriving corporate culture.

Action Plan to Lead with Hospitality:

ENGAGE

*Transform menial jobs into meaningful
work with service and engagement.*

We have now reached the end of Part Three—ENGAGE. Here are this section's prompts and exercises to start leading with hospitality. If you like, you can write in this book. Or grab a notebook or fire up your computer and open up a new document.

Create a culture of belonging on your team and in your organization.

Be kind and intentionally *give* your time, talent, and heart to those you lead.

- *List three ways you can give your time to your team and how that will help them improve, succeed, and feel like they belong. For example:*
  - *Arrive early, and prepare how you'll engage with people each day.*
  - *Be present, in the areas, with your teams when it matters most.*
  - *Offer assistance, working alongside them, teaching, and coaching along the way.*
  - *Prepare for and commit to connecting with each individual in your one-on-ones.*

    — *Prepare for and facilitate productive and collaborative team meetings.*

_____

_____

_____

+ *List three of your strengths and how you can give them to your team, and describe how that will help them feel more comfortable and confident in their role and on your team.*

_____

_____

_____

+ *List three ways you can give your heart to your team and show them you care—and most importantly, whom and how it will lift them up.*

_____

_____

_____

Leverage the power of encouragement by recognizing people's talents and uniqueness, reminding them of their accomplishments in the past, and providing assistance where and when they need it.

+ *List one person on your team who deserves some recognition. Identify how you'll recognize this person, when you'll deliver the recognition, and the impact it will have.*

_____

_____

_____

+ *List another person on your team who may be feeling down. Identify a success or past accomplishment of theirs you can point out to them and the impact that will have on their mindset, confidence, and comfort level.*

_____

_____

_____

+ *List yet another person who may need some help or assistance understanding their role, executing their role, or simply understanding how their role ties to your organization's success. Identify when you'll carve out time with this person, craft your message of encouragement, and explain the impact this will have on their mindset.*

_____

_____

_____

_____

_____

PART FOUR

INSPIRE

Chapter 8

IMPORTANCE

Once People Feel Significant, They Lean In, Step Up, and Deliver Their Best

Pretend that every single person you meet has a sign around his or her neck that says, "Make me feel important." Not only will you succeed in sales, you will succeed in life.

—Mary Kay Ash

Mark Sanborn, the *New York Times* best-selling author and a member of the Speaking Hall of Fame, was once kind enough to hire me to speak to several audiences on his behalf, teaching his leadership-development principles and content.

The day before one of his keynote addresses in Las Vegas, he invited me to his hotel suite at Caesars Palace. The objective of our meeting was for him to share important nuances to delivering a great keynote speech. He taught me how to strategically construct a message and deliver it. In the brief yet impactful hours we shared, I benefited from his lifetime of learning, living, teaching, and speaking about how to be a great leader.

One of Mark's pearls has always stuck with me. "What's the first job of a leader?" Mark asked, as he paused from pacing and peered out the window for a moment, watching the endless stream of taxis, pedestrians, and flickering Vegas electronic billboards.

"Uh. Um. Well. I don't know. Selecting the right people?" I said, trying not to blow it. This was Mark Sanborn, my favorite author and Hall of Fame speaker, entrusting me to speak on his behalf.

"Nope," he said.

Awesome. I blew it.

"Come on. You know this," he said, encouraging me.

"Well, okay. Um, how about *being inspiring?*"

"Nope." Mark was now winking and grinning. "The first job of a leader is to prove significance. Because unless or until people feel significant, they won't even come close to making significant contributions."

"Ahhh, got it. Makes complete sense!" I said writing the word *significance* feverishly in big, bold letters in a notebook.

I've always remembered that essential principle. One of the final pieces in the puzzle of *leading with hospitality* is embracing your ability to make people feel important. So far, we've discussed two vital pieces—making people feel *welcome* and *comfortable*. These two components relate to your ability to maximize productivity, enhance your team's culture, and ultimately drive desired business results.

Without those first two components, the final piece is hard to layer into the mix. Why? Few individuals, let alone teams, are likely to be compelled to step up, sacrifice, put in the extra effort, or most importantly, conjure up the *stick-to-it-iveness* essential to battle through adversity unless they feel welcome and comfortable. Remember: we're all human, and this is simply human nature.

However, if you're successful at making people on your teams feel *welcome* and *comfortable*, making them feel *important* fits organically as a natural next step. As the speaker and author John C. Maxwell has put it, "Every person has a longing to be significant; to make a contribution; to be a part of something noble and purposeful." Plus, it propels your teams into the next hemisphere of productivity, fulfillment, growth, success, and results.

Make Them Feel Important

I mentioned earlier some similarities between sales and leadership. The common denominator between the two is trust. Before trust is built, or as some would say, before we "cross the river of trust," very little action or change of behavior will occur. After all, both sales and leadership exist to influence, guide, and change specific behaviors.

With each passing day, as you intentionally lead with hospitality, one conversation and one genuine act of kindness at a time, trust is being built. You're slowly but surely building an unsinkable, self-propelling raft that will transport you across to that highly sought-after shore on the other side of the "river of trust" with your teams.

+ You've **accepted** people for who they are rather than for *what* they've accomplished.
+ You've taken strides to fully understand them and the depths from which their own opinions, thoughts, and feelings originate. You've practiced **empathy**, and they're starting to feel something far different than they've felt about any leader before.

- You've **served** them as if they were guests in your home, making it all about them, not about yourself.

- They feel more **welcome** working with you than in any other organization or with any other leader before. People on your teams are finally starting to relax. They have an open mind, their anxieties have subsided, and they're beginning to enjoy work for the first time in a long time.

- You've proven through your generosity and consistency one conversation at a time, that you're both **genuine** and **kind** in everything you do for your team and those around you. They know it's not phony or an act. You're real, and they believe this about you. They've seen it play out, firsthand, time and time again.

- You've **encouraged** them by recognizing their strengths and by reminding them of past accomplishments, their opportunities, and their incredible potential tucked away deep down inside, waiting to be unleashed into the world around them. When they've needed it, you've stepped in and helped them through a tough season, project, or assignment.

To paraphrase Anna from Disney's *Frozen, for the first time in forever*, people on your teams truly feel **comfortable.** Moreover, they not only feel more comfortable with you as their leader and with their teammates, but also more comfortable in their own skins.

They've engaged in more conversation with coworkers than ever before, which has sparked their curiosity and sense of discovery to learn new ideas and perspectives. With each meaningful conversation between you and their peers, productive working relationships have blossomed. People working on your team and in your company feel they belong to a community worth serving and supporting.

Now, you must make them feel important. Once they begin to feel important, look out. You know they're talented, and you fully understand their capabilities. Now, it's time to ignite the spark, making sure everyone understands and believes in his or her own special, unique talents they bring to the table. Turn their potential into real action. As they begin genuinely feeling their value and importance to you and to the organization, you'll see their confidence level increase. As they feel more confident, their thoughts will turn into purposeful, intentional action.

Productivity like this leads to profitability. They begin to see and feel the fruits of their labor; the physical, emotional, and financial return on their time, energy, and passion invested in your team's cause. They have become inspired by your leadership that is inspired by simple, old-fashioned hospitality.

To really understand why it is so crucial to make your team *feel* important, consider what happens when individuals feel insignificant within a team. How many times have you seen this in action or even felt it yourself? As mentioned earlier, we're all people. We have that in common, which means we all have real feelings and thoughts. We've likely all experienced a boss, coach, or leader who made us feel about two inches tall. On the other hand, nobody's perfect. Perhaps we've all inadvertently made someone else feel insignificant. Whether it was intentional or unintentional, chances are, everyone's been on both sides of this human equation.

The Story of Sally and Significance

I had a leader once who was based out of the corporate office. We'll call her Sally. I had been on board about six months, so relatively new, yet getting my sea legs for the industry, operation, and the levers we needed to pull to move the business forward.

Sally asked me to create and deliver a presentation to multiple senior executives scheduled to visit my location in about a month. I was excited. I'd learned a great deal about our business and taken time to get to know the people on my team. I understood who was great at what, along with each person's specific areas for improvement. I constructed slides, identifying our successes, opportunities for improvement, and created some specific action plans for how we'd accomplish our senior executives' desired business results.

While I genuinely believed we could improve, our executives' desired business results had never before been accomplished in this location, based on the research I did in those first six months of conversation, observations, and analysis.

For my upcoming presentation, I included process improvement plans, SMART Goals, which we'll unpack more later (*specific, measurable, achievable, realistic, time-bound*), and a breakdown of strengths and opportunities. Everything was well prepared, and Sally approved the deck before our meeting with the corporate brass.

I was asked to block off the entire day for this time with Ricky, Sally, Fred, and Suzie. Ricky was a quantitative guy, particularly interested in the numbers. I included layer after layer of data to support my assumptions. Ricky was engaged throughout, his body language was positive, including head nodding, and at several moments, he gave verbal approval, almost "amen-ing" what I laid out. A local leader, my boss at our location—we'll call him Fred—was also engaged. He nodded and asked great questions.

As I presented, stopping to entertain questions and comments, I couldn't help but notice the momentum. With each positive gesture, I gained confidence and momentum. I felt significant. Senior Vice Presidents Ricky and Suzie had all their questions answered, and they both gave me hugs and handshakes as we concluded the meeting. With their doubts seemingly addressed, and based on their feedback, I felt it went about as well as it could have gone. We wrapped up early, and everyone had a chance to relax, get a bite to eat, and come down from our tension-filled corporate corporateness, real-life boardroom scene.

Fred, my boss at our location level, shook my hand and smiled. He patted me on the back and said, "Great job. They were pleased, and you presented very well. Well done."

After Fred's praise, I felt like a million bucks. He was always humble, appreciative, and led with hospitality. To this day, I'm convinced God had me report to Fred so I could learn what a humble, serving leader looked and felt like, firsthand.

Back in my office, I settled back into the remainder of the day. So I was surprised when Sally, my boss from the corporate office, came in and sat down.

She leaned back against the straight-backed chair. She brought up a couple issues we needed to "perfect," which my team still weren't executing to her liking. She was also one of Fred's bosses. Fred and I acknowledged her and agreed. We told Sally the issues she brought up would soon be addressed with the SMART Goals, process improvements, and specific action plans outlined in the presentation.

Sally always had to win and get in the last word. It was about power, always having the upper hand, and very little about leading with hospitality. Despite the others giving me handshakes and hugs, offering their approval, Sally couldn't let the moment last. What she said next, I'll never forget. It's a perfect blueprint for how to make anyone feel insignificant as opposed to significant.

"You still don't know what you don't know about this business," Sally said with a smirk.

I was stunned and didn't know how to respond. Ricky and Suzie, senior executives to whom Sally reported, said my presentation was great.

Fred looked at his shoes, maybe wondering why Sally would make such a comment. The presentation concluded so positively. Three minutes prior, everyone felt relieved, accomplished, and purposeful. Fred had said I crushed it!

I felt two inches tall. I mean, really? Maybe I was overly sensitive or should have seen her insecurity. Yes, I needed to learn more, but Sally made me feel insignificant in almost every situation. My significance-o-meter fell to a new, all-time low.

Every interaction with Sally included either something another branch did better than us, or she'd mention an element she once executed perfectly with no flaws when she was in my role. She was superhuman! In every conversation, I felt lower and lower, and less capable of measuring up to her expectations. I'm sure she had all six Infinity Stones.

I doubted myself as my confidence waned. Yes, much of my reaction could've been better managed by the person I saw in the mirror every morning. But, hey, I'm human. You're human too. So are the people on your team.

> In a study by researchers at the University of Pennsylvania, participants were 50 percent more productive when they felt valued and appreciated.[31]

I left that job two months later. It was a toxic environment where I felt uncomfortable and insignificant.

Purpose

Several years earlier, before my Sally-and-Fred season, I was in my office when a coworker and good friend walked in to say hello. As he walked in, I overheard some passionate dialogue between our coworkers on a sister team next door. During this time, my buddy and I were a bit down and feeling unmotivated.

I said, "Listen, they're fired up all the time. It seems like they're all dialed in, on a mission. We haven't had that kind of energy or enthusiasm on our team lately." My buddy was a few years older, which I always valued. He was wise and wicked smart.

He candidly replied, "It's because they have purpose. We don't have purpose right now."

He was right.

Their leaders engaged them in every decision and task to be completed in a collaborative manner. They also made sure each person realized what was at stake and what they were a part of creating and delivering for their guests, customers, and clients. Each person was aware of the end goal and where they were headed. Most importantly, their leaders entrusted them with responsibility for getting the organization to its destination.

When we have purpose, we know exactly who we are, where we're going, and most importantly, *why we're doing what we're doing*. This is a magical feeling—one of significance, driven by passion.

When people fully understand the purpose for an organization's existence, they buy in on a much deeper, personal level, and rally together to make it happen. It sounds simple, but it's not always easy. The very thought of purpose, the answer to the question "Why are we here?" is often forgotten and swept under the rug. Too often, it leads to teams dragging themselves to and from work rather than showing up to work with positive attitudes, feeling a sense of purpose about what they're there to do. Then leaders look around and wonder why. Usually the problem can be solved by making sure everyone is aware of the organization's overarching purpose and each person's role in carrying it out.

When cast members at Disney Vacation Club are reminded of their overarching purpose to "change people's lives" or when MGM Resorts International associates are told they exist to "entertain the human race," I'm sure they feel purposeful.

Consider this quote from the great writer and storyteller Mark Twain: "The two most important days in your life are the day you are born and the day you find out why."

Purpose inspires people to intentionally lean into their passions and natural abilities to make a positive difference. When people develop a strong sense of purpose, they do their best work because they want to, not because they have to. If our role as leaders is to inspire others to perform at their best, then ask yourself the simple question—*Will people perform better in situations where they want to do great work or in situations where they have to do the work demanded of them?*

If you want significant contributions from your team, consider the extent to which your team understands the purpose of the organization and their purpose in it. Remind them of it and make sure they understand. Create even more purpose by linking each person's individual role to your organization's overarching purpose.

Let them know that's why you chose them. Remind them you trust them as a valued member of the team. It will directly impact their output and the quality of their contributions. You'll have inspired and motivated an otherwise uninspired, unmotivated person to deliver their best work. Over time, this will result in your ability to deliver results to your senior executives, owners, or the board of directors.

Remember my boss Fred? Fred was great at giving his full interest and attention, even for a few minutes. Every day, he'd come in and engage with me. Sometimes, I'd walk into my office, and there would be Fred, just chillin' and engaging with my team. Other times, he'd sit there, waiting patiently on me. He wanted to see how everything was going and if he could help. Frequently, he'd take me to lunch to do his engaging. I loved those days.

After a while, as the weirdness of his obnoxiously awesome kindness wore off, I realized he was just genuinely interested. He wanted to help and teach, and in some cases, he made sure I was surviving the craziness of our collective grind. He was there to engage as opposed to bark out orders.

He had a way of showing me how my efforts were making a positive impact in the way each person on my team was performing. While I wasn't necessarily new to leadership, I was new to some of the nuances of this particular type of business he and I were leading. Fred showed me the tangible results, stats, and metrics that were improving among the individuals on my team; and then he linked it back to some of the simple things I was doing as their leader that he hadn't seen before. These were simple things like having conversations with people every single day, being available to help them when they needed it, and putting my "coach" hat on and teaching them some things I'd learned from past roles working in other organizations like Disney and Wynn Resorts.

Every time we parted, I always felt significant. I walked more briskly, confidently, and with purpose, back into the operation with more purpose and passion than before our chats, every single time. Most of the time, I was inspired and moved to engage with members of my team.

So be like Fred with your teams and engage with people every day. Get out of your office and visit them in their workspaces. Be genuinely interested in them, their progress, their mindsets, and most importantly, how you can help them become the best versions of themselves.

A True "Importance" Story

Jenna, a thirty-two-year-old middle manager working for a rental car company, had a tough gig. As a sales performance manager, she was in a corporate role, supporting multiple locations, managers, and frontline associates. Her role was to teach, coach, consult, inspire, and motivate associates and leaders to maximize sales.

In her industry, profitability is about price, length of rental, and add-on sales. The name of the game is to maximize revenue, minimize costs, and deliver bottom-line results. (In corporate America, this is a familiar tale as old as time.) I'm sure you relate, as your organization is most likely held to the same standard.

Frontline associates and leaders didn't report directly to her. Jenna's boss was in a regional role. Yet, everyone in those locations—with their competing agendas, priorities, strengths, weaknesses, and personal insecurities—were expected to play nice and deliver results as one team.

One day, several frontline associates and managers of one of Jenna's locations were unable to come in. This left only Jenna and the district manager of the location—we'll call him Gabe—to steer the ship for the day. This wasn't the normal routine for Jenna. She was responsible for observing, consulting, and teaching sales tactics, not necessarily leading the entire operation.

However, Gabe decided to leverage her talents, asking Jenna to switch hats for the day and run the actual operational show. His role was at a more senior level, tasked with overseeing the entire operation while communicating with his executive leaders closer to the C suite.

As you know, corporate America doesn't provide a pause button when unforeseen circumstances occur. If Gabe got immersed in running the show as part of the processes themselves, he couldn't deliver for his own executives and associates, with ample oversight and visibility into the entirety of the operation. That's why this day was the day he decided to trust his sales performance manager to captain the entire operation.

Yes, there were things Jenna didn't know, and Gabe knew she'd be out of her comfort zone. But he also knew she felt welcome in his location, because of the relationships they'd fostered with one another and together as a united leadership front to the team. He also knew she felt comfortable in her own skin, as a well-respected up-and-comer in the organization. That was enough to give her the keys and entrust her with the team, the people, the processes, and the bottom-line results.

Gabe huddled up with Jenna and gave her some overarching parameters and the autonomy to run the show. She was nervous when she arrived that morning. However, once Gabe, who wasn't even her direct boss, gave her the clipboard, keys, and captain's seat, her confidence rose.

She asked a few questions and he set clear expectations. She was honest about where she had limited knowledge.

He let her know even if she made mistakes, he'd help. Most importantly, he said, "I trust your ability to lead, inspire, and motivate the team."

He reminded her how much she'd accomplished in just a short time with the company, to boost her confidence. He gave her his schedule for the day. With a smile, he said, "It's your show. Go make us some money."

As she collected her thoughts, everything she'd learned from her district manager, her operations manager, and her area sales performance leader raced through her mind. Then it was like she flipped a switch. The lights came on, the starting lineup was announced, and it was game time.

The day was busy with many transactions, a few hiccups, and frontline associates diligently assisting customers. One transaction, one conversation, one opportunity, and one challenge came after another. Jenna leaned into her talents, skills, personality, charisma, and compassion, which shined as her own personal brand of leadership.

When the results were tallied by day's end, the sales reports reflected revenues of 150 percent of the location's average daily revenue. The district manager, Gabe, gave Jenna all the credit.

She was only two years into the job, working in a new industry with new coworkers. Yet she felt as important as the CEO because Gabe led with hospitality. He'd spent months building a solid foundation so she felt welcome and comfortable. On this day, he entrusted her with the keys, making her feel important. She still tells the story of how important she felt that day and how great she felt about herself and her team. Her confidence still radiates with every phone call, meeting, coaching session, and conversation she has with customers. Most exciting is her overflowing joy, passion, and commitment. The heart and soul she puts into her job is a result of how she feels when she goes to work.

I know the story well because that sales performance manager in the story happens to be my wife, Jenna. I've listened to her stories, seen the peaks and valleys, and watched proudly as she gives her time, energy, and commitment to her teams, leaders, and the company.

I've even seen her moved to tears when she downloads new sales reports and their bottom-line results come in well above expectations. I'm inspired by her effort and her district manager's compassion and commitment, not to mention his ability to consistently create environments in which people feel important, valued, and confident to be who they were destined to be.

Her location has a successful, profitable, and thriving culture many senior executives in the company consider to be the benchmark for other locations to emulate.

Fulfillment

When leaders engage and instill a sense of purpose, their teams begin feeling fulfilled as they carry out their masterful work. However, you'd be surprised how many leaders place creating fulfillment last on their list of priorities.

On the other hand, those who lead with hospitality keep this at the top of their list of leadership to-dos.

I can't see you or hear your feedback so far. However, it feels like we're building a strong case for leading with hospitality. Of course, our purpose is to inspire and motivate people on our teams to become the very best they can be.

Take a look at the root word of *fulfillment*, which is to *fulfill*. It means "to develop the full potential of."

Isn't it ultimately up to us as leaders *to develop the full potential of* our people?

Of course it is.

As Mark Sanborn teaches, "Proving significance may very well be our first real task as a leader."

Mark tells a short story in *The Fred Factor* that illustrates the simple yet powerful impact of this principle. He recounts an experience he had at Atlanta's International airport, at the food court.[32]

A young man whose role was to clean tables was clearing the remnants of unfinished lunches and dinners, and putting cups, plates, and trays in the trash. Then, the next wave of eaters-on-the-run would have a place to sit. Mark noticed the young man was slouched over, his head hung low. He moved at a glacial pace clearing table after table. Mark went over to him, tapped him on the shoulder, and thanked him. He told him if it wasn't for his time and effort, cleaning each table, all these people in one of the busiest airports on the planet wouldn't be able to sit and eat.

After that interaction, the young man stood a little taller. He threw his shoulders back, and with his head held high, he carried on, doing his best to make sure everyone had a clean table for their meal. He smiled and engaged random strangers while cleaning and wiping off tables and chairs. He felt significant and therefore returned to making significant contributions.

How do you think your team would grade you on the makes-me-feel-significant scale? A good exercise is to consider each person's level of work or quality of their contributions. Then, compare it with how you think they'd grade you on your I-make-them-feel-significant score. Often, we find a direct correlation. When our teams feel significant, they usually make significant contributions.

How do you make sure your teams feel significant, as opposed to the example of Sally, who seemed to always show the alternative? How do you model significance so your team members feel great about themselves so they lean in and deliver their best work?

Glad you asked.

Following are three significance sparkers to help you make sure your team feels important.

1. **Create a sense of purpose.** Discover your own purpose. Help others find their purposes. Help everyone on your team understand how their individual role connects to and supports your organization's overarching purpose.

If you're having difficulty discovering your own purpose, here's a simple exercise to find it:

- Ask yourself *what breaks your heart.*
- Ask yourself *what you love to do and what you do better than most.*
- Ask yourself *who you want to help.*
- Fill in the following *purpose statement:*

    My purpose is to *give* _____ to help _____ accomplish _____.

Live your purpose, and everyone else will become compelled to find and live their own purpose.

2. **Make sure each person knows you're aware of just how significant they are to the organization.** Remind them of their significance. Show them how important they are, every chance you get. Ask what type of work they'd like to do more of to make them feel more significant. They'll feel like a needed member of the team, and you'll see them perform to their full potential. A team operating at full potential leads to delivering an exhaustive list of results to the Freds and Sallys (and Rickys and Suzies) of the world. As you navigate these conversations,

   - be present,
   - be interested,
   - be open, and
   - be honest.

3. **Fill their cup to the brim.** You'll discover what makes them tick, gets them going, and what moves them as you engage in old-fashioned conversation with them every single day. Once you identify each individual person's motivations and inspirations, leverage those emotional connections so everyone gets to at least dabble in the tasks, activities, and initiatives that

fill their cup. Give your people opportunities to master their work. Create platforms for people to showcase their strengths and special talents.

When we make our teams feel important, cool things happen. The next three chapters will reveal ways to help your team genuinely feel a sense of importance, which translates into the level of confidence essential to take appropriate action, drive necessary productivity, deliver desired results, and, perhaps most importantly, keep individuals loyal and committed to bringing your leadership vision to life.

They'll be loyal to you because they trust you. They'll be loyal to the organization because they become emotionally invested and connected to the people, the mission, and your purpose. When talented people become committed, confident, and purposeful, the sky is the limit for their success, happiness, and contentment.

> Companies that understand the increasing emphasis of purpose in today's professional landscape improve their ability to attract such employees and also their ability to retain them for longer periods of time.
>
> —Reid Hoffman, Executive Chairman and Cofounder of LinkedIn

Apply the following three activating steps that follow to make sure those you lead genuinely feel valued and an overwhelming sense of importance as an integral part of your team's road toward success.

Put *Hospitality in Action—* Activating Importance

1. **Ask for perspective and insight.** You hired your employees for a reason. They're smart and capable, with ideas of their own. You'll make them feel important when you invite them to share their own perspectives and insights, and you'll learn some new things in the process. Remember: all of us are smarter than any one of us. It doesn't matter where ideas come from; it just matters that they're great ideas.

   For example, if you or anyone you know have ever been to Walt Disney World or Disneyland on your birthday, you may have been given an official birthday button to wear all day around the park. That idea came from a frontline security cast member, not a corporate executive. Great ideas come from anywhere, especially on the frontlines among the people doing the work that matters every single day.

2. **Trust people before you know you can.** There will never be a perfect time or a perfect moment to officially hand over the reins or responsibility. On the other hand, most people will rise to the challenge when someone gives them the opportunity. The challenge for you, as a leader, isn't whether or not they're ready. Instead, are you ready to provide them with an opportunity to spread their wings and soar?

   Consider some of the best athletes in the world, from Olympians to professional athletes. Their own coaches are never 100 percent certain they're ready for the moment. They trust them anyway. The athletes count on their natural strengths and abilities and perform. Your employees will do the same. All you need to do is *give* them the opportunity. Trust them before you know you can and watch them show you all they can do.

3. **Delegate and separate.** Once you give them the expectations, let it go, like Elsa in *Frozen*. When they know they've been left alone to complete their tasks, duties, or mission, you'll have elevated their effort, their conscientiousness, and their performance. I remember when I was working at Wynn Las Vegas during the opening of Encore, the second tower of pristine hospitality elegance on the north end of the famous Las Vegas Strip. Though it was a challenging time, my boss at the time, Tom McMahon, used to tell me often, "Delegate and separate."

Not only was I in my late twenties trying to pull of my first director-level leadership role, but we also had to operate Wynn Las Vegas at the same time we were opening Encore Las Vegas. I couldn't be two places at once, but Tom reminded me that I wasn't alone in this mission! We had hundreds of people on our team and thousands more beyond that in our sister departments across the organization.

It's amazing what a little delegation will do for your own mindset and stamina as a leader, not to mention the confidence boost it gives your team when you show them just how much you trust and value their ability to take on more responsibility and run with it.

Chapter 9

GRACE

Amazing Grace Wins Every Time

> *It's easier to remember to give grace when we remember how desperately we need grace.*
>
> —Lysa TerKeurst

While we can do many things to make the people on our teams feel important, I'd like to expand our understanding with the concept of *grace*. You can change your team's mentality by practicing a little grace when it comes to forgiving mistakes and shortcomings.

There's also value in simply being graceful with your own thoughts, words, and actions, as that creates a more positive and productive environment as opposed to the alternative. People can feel the difference.

Practicing grace, especially when people don't expect it or when they may not deserve it, absolutely will make them feel important. It's extraordinary and special. The word *special*, by definition, sparks good feelings and sentiments. These include positive words such as *remarkable, exceptional, significant,* and not the least of which, *important.*

When we're graceful with our actions, our words, our gestures, and our demeanor, the entire team feels uplifted. In the absence of grace and a graceful demeanor, people feel their hard work and all their efforts are cheapened.

They'll begin looking for greener, more graceful pastures.

For example, if a leader uses foul language, is abrasive, and at times exhibits borderline verbal abuse when inevitable adversity creeps up, others begin to follow suit. They begin to think that type of behavior or demeanor is acceptable. In an abusive and toxic work environment, it's nearly impossible for people to feel important about themselves or their situations. In those moments, it becomes even harder to drum up the energy, enthusiasm, and passion to give their best.

I once had a leader who referred to my team as "pansies." Though she never said it directly to them, she said it to me. That's not exactly graceful. It became increasingly difficult to take her seriously. As time progressed, it became more and more difficult to take the company and its corporate executives seriously. The company itself started losing credibility in my mind all due to the actions of one leader. All I could think about was how unimportant I felt working in an environment for so-called leaders who carried themselves in such a way.

This is a choice leaders make. We have two choices when our teams and individuals on them come up short. When they lack consistency, heart, drive, passion, commitment, or productivity, we have a choice regarding how best to deal with it.

You can try to come off as superhuman and cut them down, verbally bashing people, berating them via email, and leading through power and fear. That's certainly one route. Or you can be human, realizing the people you're leading are just that; they're also human beings. You can practice a little grace and compassion and meet them where they are, reconnect, regroup, and lift them up.

The superhuman route, as I've alluded to, is frankly shortsighted. It might make you feel powerful and purposeful in the short-term, as you pull rank, prove your point, and "win" a conversation. However, it's unsustainable. Perhaps more importantly, it doesn't transform, lift up, or inspire the right actions you need from your team over the long haul. In fact, it belittles people on your team and shows you in a negative light among your own peers and leaders.

Leaders who lead with hospitality are in it for the long haul and the long game. They take the time necessary to connect, reconnect, teach, and reteach, while making sure people continue to feel important despite their mistakes.

Nobody is perfect. I'm not perfect. You're not perfect. They're not perfect.

Leaders who lead with hospitality don't expect perfection. They inspire the levels of activity, productivity, commitment, and passion that lead to progress. When people see and feel progress, they feel important. When people feel important, there they go, leaning further into who they are and what they bring to the table with confidence.

Once again, that's the goal of leadership—*to inspire and influence people to grow and change for the better, maximizing their potential.*

Graceful Actions

If you look in the dictionary for the word *grace*, you'll discover several synonyms and descriptors that help you to understand what this concept is all about.

As a noun, *grace* means "a simple elegance, poise, finesse, agility, and nimbleness." As a verb, it has synonyms such as *dignify*, *distinguish*, *honor*, *elevate*, *upgrade*, and *enhance*.

These are also ingredients for leading with hospitality. Think about it. These words, sentiments, and most of all, feelings are a collection of descriptors many of us would use to describe our ideal boss, leader, or mentor. Wouldn't you rather follow someone with *elegance*, *poise*, *finesse*, and *nimbleness* over a person who's tactless, unforgiving, inept, crude, or downright rude, and who can't adapt to changing situations? Wouldn't you feel more compelled to go all in and crush it for a leader whom day in and day out honors you, enhances your life, and elevates you, literally upgrading your career potential with every conversation and interaction?

Of course, you would.

When a leader is refined, elegant, distinguished, and honorable in how they work, talk, walk, and lead, others will simply follow. Often, it's evident. As the leader goes, so goes the team. People will feel far more important working for a graceful leader than the alternative. When they feel important, they'll have more confidence. When they feel confident, you'll get their best work. As a leader, when you get the absolute best from everyone on your team, you're simply executing and holding up your end of the bargain.

Generous Explanations

I heard a story in church years ago about a couple who had been married for over fifty years. They had been asked how in the world they stayed together—and in love—for so long despite each other's faults, habits, and hang-ups.

The husband responded, "For everything the other person does with which you may not agree on the surface, simply come up with the most generous explanation for what they've said, what they've done, or what they haven't done, accept it as the reality of the situation, and move on."

I think this response is amazing, and it perfectly illustrates the concept of grace in action. Look at the world of hospitality for other examples. Dining out at restaurants, when we ask servers or bartenders to repeat the specials for the third time, they don't get angry; they simply repeat the specials. When you oversleep or take extra time checking out of your hotel room, staying beyond your 11:00 AM checkout time, the housekeeping or front desk teams don't come to your door with the hotel rule book and kick you out; they simply assume you're dealing with something, and they know you'll be out as soon as you can.

They serve you anyway.

They may be annoyed, but they seemingly do what the husband from the long-time married couple did for decades. In their minds, they instantly come up with the most generous explanation for why a guest is a certain way, and they serve anyway.

That's hospitality.

In chapter 6, we established *leading with hospitality* is certainly about being generous with your time, talents, and strengths in the context of inspiring, encouraging, and motivating others to be their best. It's also about giving the benefit of the doubt, with generous explanations of why or how your teams fall short.

People make mistakes. They will be inaccurate, less than productive, and inefficient, and sometimes, they'll even be mean. It's easy to take it personally, especially after all you've done and continue to do, setting out to make those same people feel welcome and comfortable.

What if they're inaccurate because they weren't trained properly? What if they're less than productive because they've lost all confidence in themselves and they're looking for guidance and inspiration from you? What if they're inefficient because they've never had a mentor or teacher show them how to structure their process? What if they're being mean to you or their peers because they're scared to death about something terrible happening at home?

Now think about how important they'll feel when you seek to understand and accept some responsibility for tending to their needs. Perhaps they've had other bosses or past leaders who were always too busy. Maybe they have trust issues because they've never felt this type of acceptance and love, let alone leadership.

You can be the leader they've never had before, but whom they've always needed to get them over the hump. Talking down to them and kicking them while they're down only pushes them further away. Come up with the most generous explanation for their actions or lack thereof. Step up and take personal responsibility to do whatever you can to help them. This kind of grace makes you a leader worth following.

Forgiveness

I know it's not Sunday school, but *forgiveness* is definitely worth mentioning in this chapter focusing on grace. In business and at all levels of leadership, we see our fair share of disagreements, arguments, and unfortunate altercations. Sometimes, it gets heated, tempers flare, and words pop out. It's often difficult to get the toothpaste back in the tube, so to speak.

As leaders, we're often at a crossroads, with an important choice to make. You can hold a grudge, skip the meeting, become nonresponsive, uncommunicative, and freeze out the people who have upset you. Or you can lead with hospitality. You can forgive, be the bigger person, take the high road, and work on mending the relationship. Your grace in these moments will be magnetically attractive, making the other person feel important.

When a leader steps up and forgives a mistake made by someone on their team, the person who fell short is touched. Truly, genuinely touched. Earlier, we hit on the importance and impact of emotional connections with brands and leaders. Offering up forgiveness when people don't deserve it is the epitome of grace. It's also a surefire way to cultivating emotional connections among people and relationships on a team. In this context, unraveling what it means to *lead with hospitality*, forgiving others is perhaps the greatest way to make them feel important.

In a moment of defeat when they feel awful about themselves after falling short—whether it was a misstep, an argument, a missed goal, a bad email, a terrible day, or an out-of-character act—the feelings of guilt can be smothering. You know how it is. The reality is even though they made a mistake, chances are, you or I have either made the same mistake before, or we've done something even worse!

Keep in mind that a mistake isn't the end of the world. In fact, the ancient root of the word *mistake* is a term from the sport of archery that means a person simply "missed the mark."

So, humbly let them know. Yes, they missed the mark this time. But it's okay to not be okay all the time. It's certainly okay to *not be perfect*. If you help them to learn from it, so they grow in some way, shape, or form, then it's all good. You've served them well as their leader.

I'll never forget a moment of grace I once experienced as a bell services manager, overseeing an extremely high-volume valet operation. Someone on my team, whom we'll call Chase, had misplaced the keys to a brand-new Mercedes Benz during a very high-profile event being held at our resort. When we realized the keys were missing,

I'll be honest, we certainly had a little moment of panic. However, in that moment, I couldn't help but notice how genuinely concerned and committed Chase was to finding these keys. The longer we looked, the more panicked Chase became.

Despite our best effort, we never found the keys to that gorgeous Mercedes. A few years earlier, a similar situation happened when we'd lost a guest's luggage. Though it was awkward, embarrassing, and very uncomfortable in the moment, I'd worked with my team and the guest to make it right with some generous guest-service recovery and out-of-the-box solutions. So I knew the same could be possible with this missing-car keys situation.

I let Chase know that we would make this right for the guest, no matter what. I reminded him that while it certainly is not ideal, these types of things are actually opportunities for us to put our *hospitality hats on* and make some magic. I also made sure he knew I wasn't mad or disappointed in him. I told him a few stories, in that moment, of times when I'd messed up, made mistakes, and caused problems in my past roles—like the time I accidentally spilled an entire bucket of oil on the boardwalk at one of the resorts at Walt Disney World, which led to them completely rebuilding an entire section to maintain the quality standards! It was totally all my fault. My leaders at the time showed me grace in that moment. Now was my time to do the same, as Chase's leader.

I met with the guest, honestly explained that, despite our best efforts, we could not find his keys. However, as a team, we came up with some magic. To get the guest home, we paid for a car service to drive him two hours to his residence. We contacted a local Mercedes dealership, gave them the vehicle information, and paid for them to create a new key. We also offered the guest a complimentary two-night stay with a food-and-beverage credit to return to our resort and obviously pick up his car with his newly created keys.

The guest was blown away with our honesty and generosity. Chase rallied his teammates, and that very day, we made some significant changes to our processes to ensure this wouldn't happen again. Above all, Chase felt important, as we all showed him grace; but perhaps the best feeling of all was when Chase saw how appreciative and forgiving the guest was for his hospitality.

Point to experiences or circumstances in your past or someone else's past when despite a misstep, everything worked out. Those on your team will be comforted, and they'll feel important as a result of your grace in that situation. That kind of compassion leads to new realms of connection, trust, and respect. Those are the building blocks for inspiring people to give of themselves—their time, talent, and skills—over and above the call of duty. They'll run through a brick wall for you when you acknowledge the mistake and reassure them everything will be okay and remind them that this mistake is only a blip on the "big screen, full-length animated feature" that is their life. Once again, you'll have inspired their best effort next time around by making them feel important with your grace.

Insecure managers focus on winning the conversation in the moment, but dynamic leaders who lead with hospitality focus on connecting with and inspiring hearts and minds as part of the long game.

Last Chance U

Last Chance U is a Netflix docuseries that chronicles life in big-time community college football. I had no clue the extent to which *community college football* is a thing until I sat down and watched it. It's literally one real-life story after another about some of the most talented, physically gifted college football players in the country. Some may have been kicked off their Division One teams the season prior for violating team rules. Other athletes were arrested for some infraction, causing their dismissal from a big-time college football team. Some players have come from unsupportive families, and others grew up in and out of foster care, fighting for their lives on the streets of the city where they were raised. Whether they're from rural or urban areas, a football scholarship for many of these student athletes is their only way out of poverty.

Many of these athletes are gifted and talented enough to one day make it and play football in the NFL. However, unless they can showcase their talents in game situations at the collegiate level and get their academics back in order, they'll never get that opportunity.

They could easily end up on a much different life path. So, a stop in community college helps them regroup and get their life, their academics, and their game cleaned up so they can move back to the Division One level on a football scholarship.

The first two seasons of *Last Chance U* showcased Eastern Mississippi Community College (EMCC), located in Scooba, Mississippi. The Lions of EMCC are a perennial powerhouse team, always among the nation's winningest teams at this level of football. The head coach is Buddy Stephens, the quintessential fiery coach, with a strong Southern accent. In season one, every other word was mothereffin' this and mothereffin' that. He beat his players up verbally at every practice and game. He was relentless. It was painful to watch him. With each episode, we watched him gradually lose the respect and trust of his team members.

There was one regular season game remaining before the playoffs in the 2015 season. At a game against Mississippi Delta Community College, an all-out, bench-clearing brawl broke out. Nearly all the players and coaches on both sides rushed the field, throwing punches trying to protect their teammates.

Coach Stephens made a huge scene on the field, with the officials and the opposing team's head coach. As the fight finally broke up, he was yelling, screaming, and nearly got thrown in jail. The rest of the game was called off, and the EMCC Lions were given a three-game suspension.

Coach Stephens's pride and superhuman attitude ultimately ruined the team and cost several players a chance to receive the Division One scholarship they'd journeyed all the way to Scooba, Mississippi, to earn.

However, that wasn't the worst part. The worst part was when Coach Buddy Stephens screamed at his players in the locker room after the game, calling them "rednecks" and "thugs." At that point, players began to physically stand up and walk out of the locker room, losing all respect for their coach, the leader in whom they'd placed their trust for one last chance. The irony was that, just a few weeks prior, Coach Stephens had been suspended for two games for pushing a referee! Not graceful behavior in the least.

As a result, during the season his team lost focus and mentally checked out, and they felt about as low as they'd ever felt in their lives. Believe me: these young men hadn't exactly led fairy-tale lives. And at this moment, they didn't feel important at all.

Coach Stephens watched that first season of football on Netflix along with the rest of us. By his own admission the following season, he didn't like what he saw on the screen. In fact, he was appalled.

Season two was different. Coach Buddy Stephens made a big change. Because he changed, his team changed. Because the team changed, the vibe changed, and the culture changed. Individual and team results also changed for the better.

While he didn't magically transform into a perfect, model citizen, in the first few episodes of season two, Coach Stephens cleaned up his mouth, drastically reducing his foul language. In fact, as a way of holding himself accountable, every time he said a bad word, he'd get down into the grass on the field and do five push-ups. Most of the time, he spoke more softly. He replaced his relentless berating with uplifting encouragement. When the team messed up, he coached, taught, and showed them grace with his genuine love for them and concern for their futures.

Players started lifting each other up, loving each other up, and pumping each other up with a newfound sense of hope for the future.

Assistant coaches began talking, walking, and coaching with more grace than before.

They focused on helping these young men get to the next level in football and in life.

Toward the end of season two, for weeks, things were on the up and up. The culture was changing, and young people were getting into a groove, learning, growing, and succeeding on the field. However, as pressure mounted in the final weeks of the season, Stephens's pride got in the way, and his harsh way with words, short temper, and less-than-graceful demeanor returned. With each brutal, verbal bashing and contentious comment, we watched relationships unravel again, and the culture fell apart.

At the end of the season, most of the assistant coaches left for greener, more graceful pastures, coaching elsewhere. The Lions' academic advisor, Brittany Wagner, left her role after eight years. She couldn't handle the negative culture another minute. Fortunately, because the culture was on the up and up for several weeks earlier in the season, several athletes made enough progress in the classroom and on the field to lock in scholarships to Division One schools the following year.

That was the saving grace of the season.

Coach Buddy Stephens was honest afterward about how he felt watching himself on TV again. He said he didn't like the man he'd become. Nor did he approve of his own actions, language, and demeanor. I love that he was adult enough and responsible enough to admit he needed to change and become more graceful. Despite all the drama, his humanity was impactful, which makes us all stop and think.

Your Own Leadership Docuseries

Consider what a real-life docuseries chronicling your leadership life would look and sound like if you watched yourself on screen like Coach Stephens did. Imagine you knew thousands, maybe millions of people had watched along with you. Would you approve? Would you see yourself being graceful, helpful, and encouraging people on your teams? Or would the film reveal areas in which you were overly harsh, brash, abrasive, or unforgiving at times?

If you watched yourself back on video, would you want that person as your own leader?

Be graceful and intentional about showing grace to people on your teams. Nobody is perfect. So guard against expecting perfection. Inspire progress with your genuine, graceful encouragement. That's leading with hospitality, and it will be well received every time you give your true, authentic heart to your team.

Put *Hospitality in Action*— Activating Grace

1. **Extend grace.** Generous explanations can save you from an otherwise downward spiral of frustration, worry, and perhaps worst of all, regret. When we come up with the most generous explanation for why others fall short, we guard against momentary flare-ups of pride that can ruin relationships and teams.

   In doing so, we allow the person on the receiving end to feel about as important as they've ever felt. The grace we've extended is both rare and moving. Trust will continue to take hold when grace takes a front seat. Those people on your team will be moved to move in the direction you need them to go, and sooner versus later, you'll lead them to exactly where you want to take them.

2. **Ask for and receive grace.** Remember: great leaders aren't great as a result of their leadership-ness. They're great because of their humanness. No one is perfect, not even great leaders. When you need more time, a second or third chance, and especially when you make a mistake, simply ask for a little extra grace.

   When you're humble enough to ask your team, your own leaders, or your partners for grace, it doesn't make you less of a leader. It makes you more human. You'll make others feel important when they realize you're every bit as human as they are and you trust them enough to let them in on your mistakes as much as your successes.

3. **Be graceful.** Graceful words, graceful actions, and graceful hearts create environments where people feel safe, both personally and professionally. When people feel safe, a sense of belonging replaces the awkward alternative. When people feel they belong, they feel important.

When people feel important, they perform at their absolute best. When people perform at their absolute best, we've done our jobs as leaders. At least for today. Tomorrow, we start again.

Chapter 10

PLANNING AND COACHING

Strategic Planning Charts the Course, and Effective Coaching Steers the Ship

If you don't know where you are going, you might wind up someplace else.

—Yogi Berra

When leaders pause their own work, breaking from their calls, emails, analysis, preparation, and meetings to spend quality time with people on their teams, it's very special. It's special because it makes people feel special and important. The only thing better is when leaders take the time to teach and coach people on their teams—but it, too, is an opportunity that leaders often miss.

Simple Planning Goes a Long Way

This chapter expands on the impact you'll make when you help your teams with the crucial, but often missed exercise of *strategic planning* and *coaching*. If executed in a timely and appropriate way, this simple principle can be the difference between leading individuals or teams to success versus letting them slide down a path toward failure. Leaders who lead with hospitality, genuinely putting others first, have a knack for making people feel important. The more we learn, the more knowledge we have. With every dab of additional knowledge comes an incremental feeling of, you guessed it, *importance*.

Before diving into how to help our teams with strategic planning, I must share a quick hospitality story that illustrates the impact of helping people with this critical but often missed leadership exercise.

Your Personal Disney Vacation Club Guide

Having grown up as a Disney kid with my parents taking us on vacations to Walt Disney World throughout our childhood and teenage years, naturally, I wanted to work for Disney when I grew up. This became the foundation of my fascination with all things hospitality from a very early age. As mentioned earlier, I interned at Walt Disney World each summer in college. Following graduation, I worked in several hotel operations leadership roles as well as sales leadership roles for Walt Disney Parks and Resorts in Orlando, Florida.

Later, I was blessed with the opportunity to lead the sales team for Disney Vacation Club, based at the Disneyland Resort in Anaheim, California, during a period of rapid growth and expansion. During my time at Disney Vacation Club, we opened a second sales-and-preview center at Disneyland and two new Disney Vacation Club Resort properties within a thirty-six-month span. It was quite a ride.

My first day on the job at Disney Vacation Club, a tall fellow *popped* into my office. (Salespeople absolutely master the art of the pop-in office visit, I soon came to find out. If there was a Hall of Fame for office pop ins, all salespeople would be first ballot hall of famers.) He was rocking a Disney tie, Disney socks, a perfectly pressed dress shirt, and a classic Disney persona, smiling ear to ear. He stood about six feet three inches tall, so he had a couple inches on me. He introduced himself, extending his hand to shake mine while holding a piece of paper in his left hand.

His introduction went like this: "Hi. I'm Andy, one of the Guides here. It's very nice to meet you. I just wanted to welcome you to the team, and if you'll just sign right here, we'll get your credit application started so I can help you buy some Disney Vacation Club points!" Mind you, I was his new boss, and this was literally day one.

He was only half kidding. I loved his sense of humor right out of the gate. I knew he undoubtedly had to be a great salesperson and a leader among his peers on the team. It was a great way to break the ice in an otherwise awkward situation, as I embarked on a new leadership role with a well-established, veteran team.

Andy was by far the most successful DVC Guide on the Disneyland team and one of the top DVC Guides in the entire system, spanning Walt Disney World, Disneyland Resort, Disney Cruise Line, Aulani, a Disney Resort and Spa in Ko Olina, Hawaii, and the tele-sales team.

Prior to joining Disney Vacation Club, Andy's career was both dynamic and impressive. He hailed from Allentown, Pennsylvania, and was a two-time alumnus of the University of Pittsburgh; a Pitt Panther holding both undergraduate and graduate degrees in business. Prior to DVC, he was a finance executive with Ford Motor Company and the chief financial officer of three startups that he ultimately helped exit with successful buyouts to larger entities.

I loved working with him and learning from him, and most of all, I loved watching him work. It was poetry in motion and a perfect blend of art and science in how he set out, genuinely leading with hospitality in his role.

Many characteristics and qualities set him apart from the pack. Like many great brands, companies, or even leaders, it wasn't one thing or a magical silver bullet that made him successful. The opposite was and still is true about Andy. It's the combination of a hundred little things that made him a great Disney Vacation Club Guide. For the purposes of this illustration, in the context of leading with hospitality, I'll zero in on how Andy helped his prospective and current Disney Vacation Club members *strategically plan* out how they would use their membership. His approach to sales was more like teaching and coaching rather than selling.

It started in his initial dialogue with guests as he hosted their introductory DVC tour or phone call. Leaning into his role in the show as a Guide (Disney always capitalizes that!) he embodied everything we loved about our favorite teachers growing up. (Side note: If you happened to visit Andy's personal Facebook page at the time, he listed his occupation as "Teacher at Disney Vacation Club.") Before he taught, he spent quality time discovering all he could about the person or family in front of him.

In the *exploratory phase*, Andy didn't stop asking questions or peeling the onion until he discovered the following:

+ What were their goals for the membership?
+ How frequently would they use the membership?
+ When would they use the membership?
+ Why do they need the membership?
+ Where would they use the membership?
+ What problems would a vacation membership solve?

During the discovery process a few things happened simultaneously. He learned more and more about them and, most importantly, he learned what they needed and why they needed it. In short, he discovered the problem he could help them solve. While Andy was learning, his new friends and prospective Disney Vacation Club members were also discovering their problems. They began to understand what it might look and feel like if they took the plunge and joined Disney Vacation Club. Andy led them down a path of self-discovery like a true, genuinely interested leader or teacher.

Something else was happening at the same time. With each carefully crafted question, taking a genuine interest in how he could help them (not sell them), Andy's guests often became the newest members of the Disney Vacation Club, and they began to feel important.

All their fears, worries, and anxieties dissipated along with every negative timeshare connotation they probably carried with them into the tour. This person, this Guide they'd only just met, was more focused on helping them than anyone in their lives up to that point.

Next, Andy would progress and begin *teaching* them. Once he fully understood their goals and needs, he taught them *how* Disney Vacation Club could help fill the void in their current situation, solve their problems, and add value to their lives in ways he'd just learned they both wanted and needed.

He also taught them how to use their new membership strategically. It's a complex membership with a point matrix, multiple seasons, many villa types and sizes, different tiers of resorts, and varying destinations for which the needed quantities of points differ from one scenario to another. Members can bank their points to the following year, borrow points from the next year, and even rent points if they need an odd, random quantity to fulfill a specific vacation!

It can make your head spin, but it truly is a life-changing experience to become a Disney Vacation Club member; and those of us who are members certainly have priceless memories and magical stories worth telling of time spent with our families.

To put it in perspective, an entire team included hundreds of Cast Members stationed and scheduled on phones in call centers and in online chat rooms. Each one is ready and waiting to answer questions, solve issues, and field complaints 365 days per year to support the gargantuan, tedious, and often misunderstood Disney Vacation Club experience.

Luckily for guests, prospective members, current members, as well as Disney Vacation Club leaders and executives, Andy always led with hospitality. He taught his guests and members *how* to strategically plan their vacations, *how* to efficiently and effectively use their vacation points from year to year, and he even called to remind them when to bank their points at the appropriate times.

Imagine how important his members felt when they sat across from him in a suite or bungalow, and he's straight up teaching. (Another side note: My mom was my kindergarten teacher, one of my grandmothers was my fifth-grade math teacher, my other grandmother was a high school biology teacher, one of my aunts was an English teacher, and my other aunt was a health and PE teacher and then elementary school principal. So I know teaching when I see it.) He helped them strategically plan where they'd go, when they'd go, and even what to do when they arrived at their destination.

New members of Disney Vacation Club left Andy with a clear understanding and a plan for how to enjoy their investment going forward, and most of all, they felt as important as ever. They'd just spent a small fortune for nearly fifty years of vacations, but they would be laser focused on *how* they could achieve their vacation and family memory goals.

Andy taught them.

I witnessed and marveled as guest after guest signed on the dotted line, trusting Andy wholeheartedly with their hard-earned money as well as their future family memories yet to be created. By the way, many only met him ninety minutes prior to their decision to join the membership. I can't tell you how many emails, phone calls, and even social media posts I had the pleasure of fielding from guests and members raving about how wonderful and important Andy made them feel.

Disney Vacation Club's mantra is "Welcome Home." Andy and many Guides who share his passion, creativity, and commitment truly bring the brand to life with how they continue to change lives every day, teaching people *how* to vacation with DVC.

Sales Is Leadership, and Leadership Is Sales

Recall our conversation earlier about the similarities between sales and leadership. Both sales and leadership exist to influence changes in behavior, as mentioned before. Just as emotions drive purchasing decisions, guess what. Emotions also drive your team's decision to change their behavior and align with your leadership vision. Great leaders understand this principle. They intentionally, passionately, and genuinely lean into their opportunity and responsibility to create emotional connections and feelings that inspire action. That's what this whole thing is about.

Leaders at all levels and across all industries can create this level of alignment, buy in, commitment, devotion, and trust when they put in the time helping their teams *strategically plan* how they'll execute their respective roles. When considering it in this context, it's hard to imagine any other way to lead.

What's the alternative? Maybe you've had leaders who simply say, "We need to hit this number. Figure it out. I look forward to an update next Thursday afternoon. Thanks."

Unfortunately, I've had those leaders as well. It's no fun. Not cool. Perhaps that's why I'm so passionate about these principles and compelled to encourage leaders to lead with hospitality in their hearts.

The difference is real and impactful, not to mention meaningful.

I can tell. You're fired up now. You're all in on helping your teams with strategic planning. What does the process look like? Simple, but not always easy. It just takes a little time, thought, collaboration, and execution to serve this up for your people.

We'll dive into it.

Help Them Set SMART Goals

We often get downstream about a mile and a half on a project, initiative, meeting, or task, and then we feel lost.

You've put in the time, effort, and thought, yet become frustrated with the lack of results or progress. Often, our teams do the same. Too frequently, it's not until the business results come in south of expectations and senior executives put everyone on tilt with their memos, questions, and phone calls that we finally sit down and build a plan. At that point, it's too late. We've missed the boat altogether.

Great leaders and those who lead with hospitality anticipate this dynamic and plan for it strategically. The first step in *planning* is setting SMART Goals that are *specific, measurable, achievable, relevant,* and *time-bound.* The SMART part is old school, originally introduced in a November 1981 issue of *Management Review* in a paper written by George T. Doran called "There's a S.M.A.R.T. way to write management's goals and objectives."[33] I'm all for fresh, new, and cutting edge, but let's face it: unless it's broken, don't fix it.

The principle of setting SMART Goals isn't broken at all. So that's the first step in learning (or teaching) how to think about game planning more strategically and proactively, as opposed to relying on knee-jerk reactions to callouts, emails, or shortfalls on monthly or quarterly reports. When you're successful in inspiring and encouraging people on your teams to set SMART Goals for themselves, their day-to-day duties and tasks become simple. It may not get any easier for them, but at least you've helped them simplify the work to be completed. They're left with a laser-focused set of clear expectations. Help them craft the two to four most critical SMART Goals on which they need to focus for the next week, month, quarter, or even year.

> According to Gallup, only 25 percent of employees "strongly agree" that their manager provides meaningful feedback to them or that the feedback they receive helps them do better work.
>
> Only 21 percent of employees "strongly agree" that their performance is managed in a way that motivates them to do outstanding work.[34]

They may have heard about SMART Goals before. Some may even have goals, in general, already. However, as sad as it is, it's highly unlikely they've ever had a leader sit down, engage in dialogue, and help them discover what they truly want to accomplish, personally and professionally.

Chances are, no leader has ever taught them how to think differently about situations, ultimately helping them set clear goals, which become roadmaps for successful lives and careers. You'll be that leader, helping them to establish their own SMART Goals. Some goals will be for growing the business, both quantitatively and qualitatively. Others will be centered around a person's self-growth.

For instance, "Increase our sales conversion by 20 percent by the end of the third quarter" is a very quantitative SMART Goal. A qualitative SMART Goal may be something like "Commit to planning and executing a team builder per quarter for the entire year and next year." Other goals may be for their personal growth. For example, "Ensure every team member enrolls in and completes one leadership-development online training course per month for all of Q4."

How Are You Spending Your Time?

Setting goals and objectives for the team, helping them think through the gray spots at a strategic level is step one. The next step is one that's often missed. This is the best way to help people become efficient and productive with their time. It seems simple enough, but how frequently do you wake up on Thursday morning, or worse, at the end of the month, wondering what in the world you did the entire week or month? It happens way too often.

Sometimes, the scariest question to ask yourself or your teams is "How are you spending your time?" It behooves us as leaders to prevent those on our teams as well as ourselves from having to cringe when that question is asked.

So far, you're gaining momentum. You've inspired your teams, helping them define SMART Goals. The next piece falls into place. It's the *tactical daily game plan* of how everyone will spend their time. Since the SMART Goals are now dialed in, everyone has a clear a picture of where they need to go. However, the how-to-get-there is often left out in thin air between a leader's lofty pedestal and the desks of those doing the work.

Not for leaders leading with hospitality.

Leaders who lead with hospitality have been there and done that. They know how it feels to be given a laundry list of to-dos and then be left out to dry like clothes fresh off the spin cycle. Be a leader who anticipates any needs, worries, anxieties, and doubts your team has. Help them design personalized game plans of how they should spend their time so they crush the goals they've set for themselves.

How amazing? How confident? How comfortable? And how important will they feel when their leader helps them outline their paths to success? About as important as guests felt when they left a Disney Vacation Club Open House experience, after learning precisely how to achieve their family's vacation goals. Your teams will feel that same level of confidence in themselves and in you as their leader. They'll also be more aligned with the mission and their role in making it happen.

Take time to help your teams come up with tactical daily game plans. They'll thank you for helping them strategically plan their days and weeks. Your senior leaders will thank you for delivering wildly successful results *and* developing, teaching, and coaching up the talented folks on your team.

This is simple, but not always easy; and it's something often overlooked. That's why I'm sharing this with you. Action plans are nothing more than a detailed list of actions and steps, which help you organize *who will do what and by when*. This becomes your daily game plan of activities and tasks that will continue to move each individual and your team toward achieving your SMART Goals and realizing your vision.

As a leader, you can turn mere activity into productivity by helping your team members devise their action plans. We spend time in our leadership-development workshops and live learning experiences on this very topic. I can see light bulbs turning on above our participants' and clients' heads as they fill in our action plan template. It's simply a spreadsheet with the following columns:

- ✦ Task—this column is a list of the specific action steps or tasks you'll need someone (could be you or those on your teams) to accomplish to achieve the SMART Goal.
- ✦ Assigned To—this column notates the person or people to whom you'll assign the action steps and tasks.
- ✦ Resources Needed—this column lists the specific tools, information, support, or resources (financial, staffing, or equipment) needed to complete the task.
- ✦ Success Measures—this column is to identify what metrics you and others will use to measure success. For example, revenue, profits, units, percent increase or decrease, and so on.
- ✦ Due Date—this column may be the most important factor in turning *busyness* into *productivity*; it holds everyone accountable to deliver on their tasks by a certain date.

The purpose of the action plan is to strategically plan out every critical step in taking the team from where you are today to achieving the agreed-upon SMART Goal. Mastering the art of crafting compelling visions and focused SMART Goals, and also creating tactical action plans, you'll be the leader among your peers and in your organization who everyone can count on to deliver results.

At this point, in the *leading with hospitality* journey, you've been intentional and purposeful about developing strong, trusting relationships with your teams. Now, they will be even more open to your direction than ever, and they'll be more willing to step up, lean in, and execute for you than ever before.

Let It Go

We're all human beings. So the tendency at this point, after helping our teams identify and set strategic goals along with their tactical daily game plans, is to hover. We tend to be control freaks, as humans. It's hard to let go!

But as leaders, we must let go.

Leading with hospitality is about delivering *an experience* and about evoking emotional connections and feelings that inspire action. It's not a good experience when leaders, coaches, or bosses hover.

When you check into a hotel and the front desk team absolutely crushes the arrival experience, they don't follow you to your room and then to the dinner reservation they helped you plan. Nor do they accompany you out to the front drive and jump in your Uber with you. They don't make sure you sightsee exactly and precisely how they helped you plan your experience.

Conversely, when the concierge helps you plan your activities, dinners, and excursions, then follows up with a genuinely interested phone call, handwritten card, or an in-person interaction in the lobby to see if you need further assistance or to simply hear about your experience, you can't help but feel important and valued. It's amazing.

When we hover, pester, and obsess, it begins to come across as micromanaging. When someone micromanages, it makes you feel the opposite of important. Instead, you feel *irrelevant, insignificant,* and *trivial.* If your goal is for everyone on your team to shut down, stop caring, pause all productivity, and literally avoid the thought of interaction with you, let alone deliver results, then by all means, micromanage the tactical daily game plans you helped them create.

That's not you. Me neither.

When we give crystal clear expectations and work alongside our teams, helping them craft their goals and tactical game plans, and then let go, magic happens.

They know you trust them. So, trust people before you know you can. This can be the boost of confidence and self-esteem people need to get into the next gear and ultimately find themselves. Then they'll believe they belong.

Great leaders know what to say, how to say it, and when to drop knowledge and inspiration, imparting wisdom to the people they lead. You become a brilliant leader when you begin to know when to stop saying or doing anything. That's the magical intersection of art and science in leadership. Leading with hospitality is understanding when it's time to let go and allow the team to do what they do.

Tough Accountability Conversations

For most, helping them craft SMART Goals and tactical action plans will not only show them you care about their success, but it will inspire them to get moving. Will there be some who need a little extra nudge? Absolutely. In every team or group of people, you'll have high performers, poor performers, and those in the middle of the pack.

If you've been leading with hospitality along the way—*connecting, striving to become your absolute best, serving, and engaging with people*—having tough accountability conversations with those you lead, or even your own peers, becomes very simple. You will have earned the right to hold others accountable. So be confident and lean into your role as a coach.

Giving feedback and coaching people on their performance can be uncomfortable the first or second time you engage in that type of conversation. However, as with most things in life, the more you practice, the more you improve.

I remember getting *coached* by a senior leader once in a tough conversation. He was holding me accountable to hold my team accountable. At the time, I was struggling with giving people feedback on their lack of effort, commitment, and overall performance. I was over indexing on giving them grace and compassion, as I'd learned so much about them and connected with them on such a personal level that I'd formed great relationships with them. That was a very good thing—don't get me wrong. However, my love and compassion for them held me back from giving them candid feedback.

My leader called me out. While he recognized my commitment to *connecting, serving,* and *engaging* with each member of our team, he told me it was time to start holding them accountable. My initial response was, "Oh, but, sir, you don't understand. I have single mothers who drive hours on end, roundtrip, to and from work. We have guys giving up time with their family to work extra hours. I love these people."

Like all great coaches, he looked right back at me and very gracefully said, "Well, then, if you love them, you owe it to them to give them feedback and coach them so they improve. You're not doing them any favors by shying away from tough conversations that you know will make them better. Why do you think I'm having this conversation with you right now? I love you, too, and I know you're a great leader, but it's my job to help you get even better."

From that moment on, I leaned into tough conversation after tough conversation in just the same fashion as he had coached me. When giving feedback and leaning in to my role as coach in that season, I would tell people what I valued about their contributions. I let them know I cared about them in that moment and about their future, which is why

I needed to point out some things and coach them on some improvements and changes they needed to make with my feedback.

I found that when feedback is delivered with care and intention to help people improve or avoid experiencing frustration, they appreciate it. Not only do they appreciate it in the moment, but also they will always have that gift of feedback, coaching, and course correction that they take with them into their future. Look at me, all these years later, recalling one simple conversation one of my leaders had with me that certainly helped me improve how I think about and deliver feedback. I respected him then, and I respect him to this day. I've also found that every time I've given feedback to my teams or my clients since that season, people respect me more as a leader and as their coach because of the way I've learned how to deliver the feedback.

The same will be true for you when you lean into your role as a *coach* for your team. Take advantage of those teachable and coachable moments. You'll change the course of someone's life and career with every pearl of wisdom you give them, as long as you deliver it with care, empathy, and compassion.

Be a leader who devotes focus, urgency, attention, commitment, and compassion helping your teams develop strategic goals and tactical game plans—and then trust them to do it without handholding. You'll undoubtedly make them feel important, special, and valued as members of your team. Those are the feelings that inspire action and lock in emotional connections to a brand, the team, the mission, and the cause you've been entrusted to lead.

Results and relationships beyond yours and your organization's wildest dreams will inevitably take shape. You will have added to the experience, creating a culture of people who feel *welcome, comfortable,* and *important.* It will begin feeling more and more like home to your team, your guests, customers, members, and clients. It will become a place and a feeling worth returning to every day for everyone involved. Those who do return will certainly have compelling stories to tell.

Welcome Home.

Put *Hospitality in Action*— Activating Strategic Planning and Coaching

A great application to help you remember to give your team support balanced with ample autonomy so they can execute successfully is the following acronym. It's the word *code* backward, **EDOC.** It stands for the following:

1. **Explain.** Set clear expectations with agreed-upon SMART Goals for the organization and for each person on your team. Spend quality time, investing in each team member. Walk them down a path of self-discovery by challenging them with questions like "What do you want to accomplish this week, month, year, or season?" Then ask, "How can I best serve you to help you get there?" This will help them plan for themselves and establish that you're for them, not against them. They'll know you'll always be there to help them, not hurt them.

2. **Demonstrate.** Physically show them how to execute specific tasks. Help them outline their tactical daily game plans for how they'll spend their time. Walk your talk. Live the values, behaviors, and actions you'd like to see from your team. When they see you doing what you've asked them to do, they'll quickly follow your lead, trusting you along the way.

3. **Observe.** Hands off! Sit back and let them execute. Observe everything with a lens for continuous improvement and development. Ask how you can help them become even better in the coming days, weeks, months, quarter, or year. Let enough time pass as you observe their process execution or lack thereof.

4. **Coach.** Then and only then do you coach. Praise where it's appropriate and only coach when they truly need it.

It's tough to say which is the most important step. Each one is a key component in the art and science of leadership. However, one thing is certain. It's impossible to coach strategically unless or until you allow your teams ample time to perform. Allow enough time to make an assessment. Over time, you'll learn where they're excelling and where they may need a little help.

Chapter 11

INSPIRATION

Why People Do More, Become Their Best, and Deliver Their Best Work

> *To handle yourself, use your head; to handle others, use your heart.*
>
> —Eleanor Roosevelt

To bring our conversation about *making them feel important* full circle, we'll dive into the concept of inspiration. When we're inspired, we think, feel, and do things with more gusto, focus, and urgency than we knew was possible.

As we've mentioned time and again, two of the most value-added effects of leading with hospitality are *evoking emotional connections* and *influencing positive behaviors* over the long haul. Inspiration is a key ingredient to both. It's worth diving into why *inspiration* is so powerful and, essentially, how to deliver it to the people on our teams and in our lives.

What Scholars Found about Inspiration

A *Harvard Business Review* article by Scott Barry Kaufman entitled "Why Inspiration Matters" reveals *why* inspiration is such a crucial component of work. "In a culture obsessed with measuring talent and ability," Kaufman writes, "we often overlook the important role of inspiration." Kaufman's article cites research by several scholars to further support his hypothesis that inspiration matters. In particular, Kaufman cites psychologists Todd M. Thrash and Andrew J. Elliott, who point out three core aspects of inspiration, which are *evocation, transcendence,* and *approach motivation.*[35]

In simple terms, *evocation* is the act of bringing or recalling a feeling, memory, or image to the conscious mind and the action of invoking a spirit. This supports our goal of creating a culture of emotional connections with each other, our teams, and even our guests, clients, customers, and communities.

Transcendence is defined as "existence or experience beyond the normal or physical level." I like this sentiment. As Thrash and Elliott point out, *transcendence* usually involves an epiphany moment of clarity and an awareness of new possibilities. If you didn't notice it before, compelling reasons to inspire our teams, as opposed to merely leading or managing them, are becoming clearer and clearer here. What leader wouldn't want his or her team to start seeing new possibilities?

Approach motivation speaks to an individual striving to "transmit, express, or actualize a new idea or vision." Thrash and Elliott say inspiration involves being inspired by something and then *acting on* that inspiration.

The activation component should excite you as a leader. After all, once you enter the dynamic realm of leadership, accepting the challenge of influencing others, your success is a function of how effectively you move people toward progress. Once you make them feel welcome and comfortable, charismatically and simultaneously, the extent to which you also make them feel important will unleash their talents, skills, and effectiveness toward delivering results beyond what you or they thought was possible. The most meaningful way to make people feel important is to inspire them.

Being inspired by your work is truly transcendent. When you feel inspired, you start believing in new possibilities. Suddenly, you find yourself in a new and higher gear, achieving and progressing beyond what you thought was possible.

For example, sheer *inspiration* compels me to study, research, and write books. Without inspiration, I might have sat on the idea for the book you're reading, never putting fingertips to the keyboard and writing it. However, inspiration has helped me experience the message from the perspective of stories, experiences, authors, speakers, and leaders, as well as people with whom I've worked or led in the past. I've taken action to put together what I hope was a value-added, enjoyable book to read, reference, and share with your teams.

I'm sure you can think of projects or endeavors in the past you've undertaken. Consider the ones that took the most work, time, resources, and thought. Chances are, the ultimate, underlying reason you took action was because somewhere along the way you were inspired to go for it.

Kaufman's article introduces Thrash and Elliott's findings about characteristics inspired people share. For example, inspired people have a stronger drive to master their work. They often possess physiological resources such as creativity, perceived competence, self-esteem, and greater optimism.

These are feelings and sentiments every leader would love their people to exude in their roles. This highlights the thread I suggest between *inspiration* and *making people feel important*. If we removed everything else from the equation, and I told you, a leader of people, there's a magical potion you can *give your team* to make them more creative, confident, productive, feel more competent, and generally more positive all around, you'd want to give that potion to everyone at the next staff meeting. Every member of every team would gladly welcome the potion, because it would give them a feeling of importance.

I've got good news. You can give this magic potion to your teams via inspiration.

Before leaving Thrash and Elliott's research, it's worth noting one more thought-provoking finding about inspiration. They found inspired people were more open to new experiences. As Kaufman's article highlights, "openness to experience" frequently came before inspiration.

This is intuitive and reinforces the idea that people open to inspiration are more likely to experience it. A leader who leads with hospitality is primed for inspiring, since you've

> Inspired employees are more than two times more productive than employees who are merely satisfied.[36]

been intentional and purposeful, making sure your teams feel welcome, accepted, and comfortable. Their minds will be open, ready and willing to be inspired to move, contributing to the team's progress as well as their own growth toward self-mastery.

In another study, Marina Milyaskaya and her colleagues found people who were generally more inspired in their daily lives set more inspired goals that were more likely to be achieved.[37]

It gets better, and I hope this excerpt from Kaufman's article will inspire you too:

> Importantly, the relationship between inspiration and goal progress was reciprocal: goal progress also predicted future goal inspiration. As the researchers note, this suggests that goal progress and goal inspiration build on each other to form a cycle of greater goal inspiration and greater goal pursuit. Finally, inspired individuals reported experiencing more purpose in life and more gratitude.

The takeaway is that inspiration ignites people to set lofty goals, while lighting a fire within to pursue progress. With more and more progress comes the urge to work harder and aim higher so those inspired people become even more inspired as progress is made. Then, they set even more goals for which they'll be in hot pursuit, and the story continues.

This is a decent little leadership tactic and an opportunity we shouldn't ignore. Inspiration is a rare fuel. The more leaders give and create inspiring environments, the more this rare, magical tank of fuel is replenished on its own! It keeps refilling its own tank the more it's deployed.

I'm sure you've known the feeling of genuine inspiration from a former leader or an experience. Undoubtedly, you've inspired someone else—a friend, a family member, a teammate, or an employee. Let's explore some actionable ideas and strategies for drumming up inspiration among our teams, with our customers, and in our communities. When you inspire, you make people feel important; and when people feel important, they begin to act, purposefully and intentionally. That's your goal as a leader, to move people to action.

Storytime

Michael Bosworth and Ben Zoldan are the authors of a 2012 book titled *What Great Salespeople Do: The Science of Selling Through Emotional Connection and the Power of Story*.[38] When I led the sales team at Disney Vacation Club, our director of sales training called me at Disneyland from Walt Disney World on a Tuesday afternoon and recommended I read this book. She was a dynamic, influential salesperson and leader in her own right, with over twenty-five years of experience in the vacation-ownership industry. When she spoke, people listened.

I was in my first year on the job, and she told me to go online at that very moment and purchase the book. I'm glad I did. The principles and insights helped me teach and coach our salespeople to improve their closing ratios. Plus, I also learned some great leadership nuggets as well. As we've touched on it a few times, sales and leadership are similar because, to be successful at either one, you must first earn the trust of others to influence a behavioral change.

In the book, Bosworth and Zoldan explain the neuroscientific reasons storytelling and emotional connections drive and influence purchasing decisions for buyers. Without getting too science-y, basically, the brain is made up of three parts:

- The reptilian, or survival, brain is the most primitive structure primarily responsible for survival functions, including breathing, blood flow, and instinctual behaviors tied to our response to danger. It's our fight-or-flight mechanism.

- The limbic, or emotional, brain surrounds the survival brain like a doughnut according to Bosworth and Zoldan. It gives mammals like us our unique capacity *to feel*. This part of the brain motivates our actions and gives us the ability to learn, remember, adapt, and change. The limbic brain allows us to be drawn to what feels good and reject what doesn't. It's also responsible for motivation and emotion. (Recall from the beginning of this book Jonathan Haidt's elephant-rider-path analogy. The limbic or emotional brain is the "elephant.")

- The neocortex, or thinking brain, presents the ability for language, abstraction, planning, perception, and the power to recombine facts to form ideas. Bosworth and Zoldan say the neocortex gives humans the unique advantage of advanced thought. (Again, from Haidt's famous analogy, the neocortex or thinking brain is "the rider" perched atop a six-ton elephant.)

The central theme throughout the book is that emotion ultimately drives the decisions we make, not logic. Though for many years the opposite was believed to be true. It was taught in sales trainings, leadership trainings, and every other "training" coming or going. Not anymore.

Storytelling is a powerful, impactful way to influence buying decisions. As stories are shared between people, the neocortex brain goes to sleep; basically, *chilling out* to prevent overthinking. The limbic system, the "emotional brain," begins firing on all cylinders. The "elephant" is magically compelled and motivated to *move*—act, change behavior, change directions, make decisions, and get into gear.

This is why one out of every four guests who find themselves in a ninety-minute timeshare presentation on a Saturday afternoon visit to a local theme park make the illogical decision to purchase fifty years' worth of vacations for tens of thousands of dollars. It's not logical at all. Their emotions take over as they daydream about time away from the office with family and loved ones, making a lifetime of memories.

Emotions drive decisions to take the plunge on everything from a large purchase or a significant change in behavior, not logic.

Effective leaders and salespeople understand this principle so they can master the art of influence. The more emotional connections leaders or salespeople can ignite, the more success they'll realize leading and inspiring people to buy into their vision. Why?

Emotions drive decisions to act, not logic.

For leaders who lead with hospitality, storytelling is also an impactful way to influence and inspire change, alignment, and action among our teams. Just as stories influence and inspire consumers to buy, they also inspire teams to buy in and follow the leader, so to speak.

Remember what leadership guru John Maxwell said: "Leadership without followers is just a long walk by yourself."

Stories to Tell

Do you recall the whole *superhuman-leader-versus-human-leader* concept that I introduced in chapter 3? Here's another great way to lean into your *humanness*, establishing and fostering emotional connections with your team. Tell them stories about past roles, situations, experiences, and lessons you've learned. When you open up, leaning into your humanness and your vulnerability, they'll slowly but surely open up to you.

Another neuroscientific thing Bosworth and Zoldan and others highlight in their work is the concept of *mirror neurons*. When you tell a story, the other person becomes compelled to tell their story in return. All the while, a firework show of sorts begins exploding inside the emotional limbic brain, which ultimately takes over, influencing decisions and inspiring action.

Think about it. How often do you open up in a conversation and unload all the details, feelings, and goings-on of your situation? Then, they jump in sharing a story about themselves in response. It's a scientific thing, not to mention a connection spark that every leader can leverage to inspire action.

As stories are shared, the *thinking brain* chills out, remember? The fear, doubt, potential misconceptions, and tendency to overthink the credibility and trustworthiness of the other person naturally begins to fade. The emotional limbic brain wakes up and says, "Whoa! Cool. This person is semi-normal, with real human feelings like me! I had no idea." Trust, credibility, and respect emerge, which creates a foundation for solid, productive, and meaningful relationships between a leader and team.

Leaders who lead with hospitality use stories as a way of sharing thoughts and ideas their teams may find inspirational. This sounds simple, and on the surface, it's a no-brainer. (Given all this "brain talk," no pun intended.) However, we get so caught up in our own organizations with our own deliverables, expectations, and tasks that we often lose sight of what's going on outside the four walls of our own companies or organizations.

When people receive an email, link, or text message from their leader to check out something another brand or leader is doing, it communicates, "Hey, I'm thinking about you. Hope this inspires you as much as it inspired me! Let's connect about it soon. I'd love to hear your thoughts."

This is a great opportunity to inspire them with a story, and another way to make them feel important. All because you shared the story with them, personally. Stories are also an inspiring, meaningful way to recognize and celebrate great performance. For example, when someone does their job the right way and knocks it out of the park with their execution, or maybe they surprise and delight a guest, customer, or client, tell everyone about it. This is especially true in our world of email, social media, internal online platforms for employees, and podcasts. There's no shortage of ways to share stories. Share stories about specific situations, how the superstar handled it, and especially the impact or outcome.

When personal stories are shared, employees and team members feel special, recognized, and important. They will intentionally and purposefully seek ways to replicate the behavior that warranted their story to be shared in the first place. Then others will be inspired to do the same.

Experiences

Stories inspire, especially when they're shared in meaningful ways. The only thing better than an inspiring story is an inspiring experience. There's a reason the travel and tourism industry is one of the world's largest, with a global economic contribution north of US $7.6 trillion. According to the National Restaurant Association, overall 2019 annual revenues in the restaurant industry in America were projected to be $863 billion.[39] According to Statista.com, revenue generated from amusement parks and theme parks in 2016 was around $20.49 billion.[40] So, whether it's travel, going out for a meal, or spending the day at a theme park, it's safe to say people love experiences!

Leaders who lead with hospitality understand this and actively seek ways to provide their teams with experiences that will inspire them. When we experience something firsthand, whether it's a theme park, great service, art of any kind, or even time spent outside our normal routine, we're pleasantly disrupted. After this disruption, new thoughts, new learning, new perspectives, new people, and sometimes even new feelings about life become top of mind. This transcendent nature of inspiration propels us to think, believe, and most importantly, *do* what we may not have thought was possible before.

It doesn't have to be elaborate. However, it must be experiential. For example, simply taking someone out of their day-to-day environment and allowing them to spend time with another team, or in a different location, can be an *experience* that inspires the thoughts and actions you want to inspire.

Remember Ralph? My former leader who took me to an Orlando Magic game? That's an experience I still remember like it was yesterday, for several reasons. It was a great game with excitement, enthusiastic play on the court, and fun times had by all. But more significantly, it also made me feel important because Ralph personally invited me. Looking back, some of the most inspiring experiences in my career have been when my leaders and organizations invested money, time, and resources for me to participate in experiences outside the day-to-day grind.

At The Cosmopolitan of Las Vegas, I traveled with the brand-marketing team to the Pebble Beach Food & Wine Festival. Sure, I worked the events, often schlepping boxes, supplies, and marketing materials, representing our brand while engaging with current and prospective partners, clients, and guests. However, it was still an inspiring experience I'll never forget. The random cab rides to and from the airport with my leaders, the dinners, lunches, and occasional cocktail with coworkers, and especially the conversations in between made the experience memorable and worth all the hard work, energy, and time we put into it.

Even experiences often relegated to the back burner like intense, comprehensive training programs that require travel or extended time away from the office can be what people value, remember, and draw on for years to come. When I worked for Disney Vacation Club, many sales leaders were sent to Orlando. We participated in a week-long training on a new sales application. All the sales leaders would need to train our own teams to use it back in our respective locations. The training was great. But the most memorable parts of the week were inspirational conversations with peers and leaders in our sister operations, team-building experiences with peers we didn't see every day, and especially time away to reflect.

I was inspired by the experience and felt important because the company personally invested in me and the team.

Think about specific experiences you can create, provide, or invite individuals on your teams to enjoy. The time, money, and resources spent can offer a huge return.

You'll see more productivity, more proactivity, and more engagement among the team. They'll have more conversations with you as their leader, and most importantly, you and the team will overdeliver on business results.

It's amazing what happens when we allow our teams to experience new, exciting things on a regular basis. They become inspired and most importantly, they feel important. That's when they become self-motivated and kick it into another gear.

Creating Self-Motivating Environments

Psychologists Edward Deci and Richard Ryan first introduced their self-determination theory in 1985.[41] It's since been tested, tried, and proven over the years. The theory suggests that people become self-determined and motivated when three universal psychological needs are met:

+ the *need for competence,* or mastery of their work
+ the *need for autonomy,* or choice in how the work gets accomplished
+ the *need for connection,* or relatedness and a sense of belonging with whom they work

Great leaders and motivators understand this about the people and teams they lead. The mark of a great leader is less about what they themselves are able to do, and instead all about what they are able to motivate and inspire *other people* to go do.

Think about the best leaders you've ever had. What made them great? Was it their words, their style, their actions, or was it all of the above? Chances are, it was less about what they did to actually *motivate* you, and more about *the environment they created.*

You can create self-motivating environments for people on your team or in your circles as well. Focus less on what you're doing and more on the experience you are creating for your team. Here are my three Cs for creating self-motivating environments—competence, control, and community.

+ **Competence:** Give people opportunities to feel competent as you challenge them to master specific tasks, abilities, or their roles.
+ **Control:** Give people a sense of control over how their work gets accomplished by allowing them autonomy to make their own decisions and work at their own paces, so long as progress is made regularly toward achieving the agreed-upon goals and objectives.
+ **Community:** Give people a feeling of belonging as you encourage them to create a sense of community every chance they

get, developing personal and trusting relationships with those around them.

Meaningful Work

Earning a paycheck for our work is great. However, there's something much better; that's making money and meaning at the same time.

Every job in every company in every industry on the planet eventually becomes mundane. Seemingly menial tasks stack up in our inbox. It's a fact of life. So, to those who accept the challenge of leadership and feel compelled to *lead with hospitality*, we have a rewarding and fulfilling opportunity before us.

As leaders of people and teams, we can and will transform sometimes-menial jobs into truly meaningful work, one story and personally crafted, inspirational experience at a time. Often, the difference between a mundane, menial job and truly meaningful work isn't necessarily a blockbuster, trillion-dollar idea or venture. It's the little things we've explored like

- *acceptance* when a person feels they don't measure up to expectations,
- *service* when they need some help,
- *empathy* when no other leader has taken time to understand their situation,
- *genuine kindness* despite a cloud of negativity and frustration that swirls in the air,
- *making them feel significant* by recognizing their brilliance, genius, and uniqueness,
- *encouraging them* during the rough patches, valleys, and down seasons,

+ *grace and gracefulness*, which calms, nurtures, and kick-starts a rebound after a mistake,
+ *strategic planning* with intentional and purposeful coaching conversations, and
+ *inspiration* through stories, experiences, and emotional connections to the mission and overarching purpose.

Leading with hospitality is less about any of these attributes delivered in a vacuum.

Instead, the combination and consistency of them over time makes the difference that matters. Meaning at work occurs when we care about the well-being and success of others even more than our own accomplishments and achievements. That goes beyond leading with hospitality. That's good, old-fashioned inspirational leadership that always has and always will create meaning, joy, happiness, fulfillment, and contentment not only in the lives of those we lead, but also in our own lives.

That's true success, as a leader and as a human being.

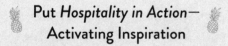

Put *Hospitality* in Action— Activating Inspiration

1. **Leverage stories.** Tell stories, write stories, share stories, and listen when they tell you stories.

    Encourage *storytelling* among everyone in the organization. Remember: *emotion* drives the decision-making process, not logic. The more we tell stories up, down, over, and across the organization, the more emotionally connected and invested everyone becomes in delivering their best to bring the vision to life.

2. **Create valuable experiences *and self-motivating environments.*** Stories spark inspiration. Experiences make those priceless moments of inspiration last in our memory for years. Seek out and encourage opportunities for your team to take part in new, thought-provoking, and comfort zone–challenging experiences. Strive to create environments in which people genuinely experience feelings of *competence, control,* and *community*.

   Minds will be broadened, and perspectives will expand. Ultimately, the bar will be raised on everyone's potential for progress.

3. **Grow yourself to grow your team.** Seek inspiration. Actively pursue opportunities to feed your mind, your body, and especially your soul. Just like successful athletes who master their craft, they don't get there by accident. They wake up every single day with a thirst and hunger to become their very best. They not only eat the right foods to get proper nutrition, they also feed their mind. Successful leaders do the same.

   Podcasts, books like this one and countless others, audiobooks, TED Talks, conferences, community groups, faith-based organizations, and even small groups with friends, coworkers, or like-minded people, pursuing self-mastery are all ways to *grow yourself* so you can *grow your team* and others. It's amazing how when you *actively seek inspiration, you become an inspiration to other people*.

4. **Create meaning.** Make it meaningful for them, utilizing one, a few, or all the tactics covered in this book. If it seems daunting

to put all twelve of these chapters and topics into action, choose only one. If you could choose to activate just one idea in this book today or tomorrow, I suggest you start by simply caring about them.

When you genuinely care about people around you and show it, even the most menial tasks transform into meaningful work. That bodes well for leading your team to success and delivering outstanding results.

Action Plan to Lead with Hospitality:

INSPIRE

*Leverage purpose and passion to inspire
your team to deliver their best effort so your
organization delivers its best results.*

We have now reached the end of Part Four—INSPIRE. These prompts are intended to help you *inspire* the members of your team. If you like, you can write in this book. Or grab a notebook or fire up your computer and open up a new document. Let's get started!

Extend grace, ask for and be open to receiving grace, and simply be graceful with your words and actions to inspire others to lean in, step up, and perform at their best.

+ *In what areas of your life or career could you extend more grace to others?*

_____

_____

_____

* *From whom could you ask for and receive grace to create a more trusting relationship?*

_____

* *How could you modify your approach, mindset, or attitude to be more graceful with your words or actions?*

_____

_____

_____

Set SMART Goals that support your overarching vision, help your teams create tactical action plans, and inspire a culture of accountability with timely and sometimes tough conversations delivered with love.

* *Craft your vision for your team or for your professional growth over the next twelve months.*

* *Set two SMART Goals for your team or for your professional growth over these next twelve months.*

_____

_____

_____

_____

* *Create your action plan for one of your SMART Goals to organize who will do what by when. (Once that one is complete, repeat until you have action plans tied to each SMART Goal.)*

Make sure everyone on your team feels significant by helping them discover their purposes and connecting their individual roles to the organization's overarching purpose.

Discover your purpose, help others discover their purposes, and show how everyone's individual purpose connects to and supports the organization's purpose. Find your purpose in three questions and a statement.

+ What are my strengths?
+ What breaks my heart?
+ Who do I want to help?
+ My purpose is to give my <u>(strengths)</u> to help <u>(whom)</u> achieve <u>(what)</u>.

Tell stories and create memorable experiences to inspire employees to do more, become more, and deliver more for your organization.

+ *Craft the story of who you are, what you do, and why you do it.*

_____

_____

_____

_____

_____

+ *Craft a story of a time when you learned a lesson the hard way, and how you learned, matured, and grew up personally and professionally from the experience.*

_____

_____

_____

_____

_____

- *Describe the best season you've ever experienced in your professional life.*
  - *What made that season such a great experience?*
  - *How did it make you feel?*
  - *How were you inspired to do more?*

_____

_____

_____

_____

_____

- *Identify how you can craft a memorable and impactful experience for someone on your team or your team as a whole.*

_____

_____

_____

_____

_____

CONCLUSION

Right now, a restaurant server is getting dressed, freshening up, and heading out the door to work. A bartender is preparing to do the same, even though she worked the closing shift last night and has only slept a few hours. A valet just reported to work at a resort hotel with much on his mind about life and his future, as he greets yet another car pulling into the front drive. A front desk person, a housekeeper, and a banquet captain are in a cross-functional staff meeting, going over the details, needs, and expectations of a massive group checking into the hotel later this week.

They're all tired. Each person has thousands of things happening in their personal lives outside of work. Today, they'll have thoughts dancing in their heads of their next day off, when they can finally do *regular life* things like get a haircut, have a relaxed meal with the family, or perhaps even engage in conversation with their spouse for more than six minutes at a time.

But they suit up, step on stage, clock in, and they're on. Thoughts about their own lives and personal concerns dissipate.

They don't do this work for themselves. They could work anywhere, but they chose hospitality.

They go to work every day to serve guests, customers, and clients.

The server explains the daily specials for the nine-hundredth time like it was his first. The bartender cuts the cocktail fruit with precision while engaging early birds at the bar as if it's opening night on Broadway and she's the star of the show.

The valet stretches, gets focused, and studies the preshift clipboard. He's getting educated about all the goings-on—arrivals/departures/special instructions/events, because he's the crucial *first impression* for hundreds of valued guests tonight.

Front desk, housekeeping, and banquets are aligned and up to speed. Their stage is set to perform a dance. Only they know the extent to which everyone has prepared, rehearsed, and perfected the choreography behind the scenes.

Somewhere along the way, every one of them has heard the line in a new hire hospitality industry orientation. "We work while others play."

It's no longer about them. It becomes about everyone else. They begin performing their art, their work, their dance and their profession, making sure everyone who visits feels **welcome, comfortable,** and **important.**

The stories guests tell when they get home aren't because of the nightly fireworks, Cinderella's castle, lakes of dreams, chandelier bars, state-of-the-art workout equipment, or the dazzling presentations to Wall Street. Instead, guests vote with their feet, wallets, and Instagram accounts because of the emotional connections sparked and reignited.

It's all about *how people made them feel.*

This is how to practice *hospitality*. It's also how great leaders lead.

When leaders realize it's not about us, but it has and will always be about loving, serving, and leading others, magic fills the air. I've seen it. You've seen it. We've also *felt it*. And we usually *feel it*, just after we notice someone practicing genuine, authentic *hospitality* in *how* they lead. These moments, though few and far between, aren't the result of what anyone says or does, but instead *how they make us feel*.

Bad days morph into good days for everyone involved. Even if it doesn't happen at first, eventually the tide will turn. Corporate culture changes for the better, when positivity replaces negativity, meaningful conversations replace gossip, encouragement replaces finger-pointing, and inspired action replaces complacency.

Results have a funny way of working themselves out over time when you lead with hospitality. As relationships are fostered, trust is built. When people feel *welcome, comfortable*, and *important*, congratulations in advance, for making both money and meaning at the same time.

Love people, early and often.

Serve people in as many ways as possible.

Lead people every day.

Lead with your words, but most importantly with your actions.

Connect. Strive for self-mastery. Serve. Engage. Coach. Inspire.

When you lead, *lead with hospitality*.

Make them feel **welcome, comfortable,** and **important.**

In the words of Maya Angelou that I shared with you way back in chapter 1, remember:

"People won't remember what you said or did, but they will remember how you made them feel."

12 Guiding Principles for Leading with Hospitality

CONNECT

1. Connect with each individual on your team by scheduling weekly one-on-one meetings.
2. Connect employees to each other and establish who will do what by when with productive team meetings.
3. Connect your team emotionally to your brand, mission, and cause with written communication, conversations, stories, and experiences.
4. Strive for self-mastery. Accept yourself for who you are, accept others for who they are instead of what they've accomplished, and accept organizational realities.

SERVE

5. Be empathetic, and always seek to understand how others think and feel about certain situations.
6. Master four fundamentals to LEAD with a servant heart: *Listen, Educate, Act,* and *Deliver.*

ENGAGE

7. Be kind and intentionally *give* your time, talent, and heart to those you lead.
8. Make sure everyone on your team feels significant by helping them discover their purpose and connecting their individual role to the organization's overarching purpose.
9. Leverage the power of encouragement by recognizing people's talents and uniqueness, reminding them of their

accomplishments in the past, and providing assistance where and when they need it.

INSPIRE

10. Extend grace, ask for and be open to receiving grace, and simply be graceful with your words and actions to inspire others to lean in, step up, and perform at their best.

11. Set SMART Goals that support your overarching vision, help your teams create tactical action plans, and inspire a culture of accountability with timely and sometimes tough conversations delivered with love.

12. Make storytelling a part of your leadership brand and team culture. Share stories of lessons learned, invite others to share their stories; and create memorable experiences to inspire employees to do more, become more, and deliver more for your organization.

ACKNOWLEDGMENTS

The book you've just read or are about to read includes thoughts, principles, lessons, stories, and applications inspired by the essence and spirit of gracious hospitality. Sure, I did the research, compiled the content, wrote several drafts, and had it in my heart for quite some time, but it took a committed and connected community to create and finalize the project.

First and foremost, I'd like to thank my wife, Jenna, whose love, support, and encouragement—not to mention patience—inspire me to give more of myself and look for the best in others.

To my parents, Jeffrey and Mary Cass Scott, thank you for loving us, supporting us, and for teaching us to appreciate hospitality experiences in resorts, restaurants, aircrafts, seagoing vessels, and everything in between.

Thank you to Matt Holt, who gave me the opportunity to work with his team and have this book published by a first-class organization.

Thank you to my editor, Claire Schulz. From our first meeting all the way through the process, you encouraged me, coached me, and inspired me with your wisdom and expertise. You made this book better. I'm very grateful.

Thank you to Jennifer Canzoneri for your advice, counsel, and leadership to promote, market, and maximize the reach of people we could inspire with this book.

Thank you to Sarah Avinger for creating a beautiful book cover and related materials to support this project.

Thank you to Shane Green, who gave me the opportunity to do the work I love to do, teaching, coaching, inspiring, and developing leaders at various organizations all across the world. All the while, you supported me and encouraged me to write this book while teaching me how to create workshops and related content to accompany it to inspire and encourage people.

Thank you to Azalee Maslow for your advice, encouragement, and partnership in creating and supporting my own personal brand as well as the Lead with Hospitality platform.

Thank you to Jon Gordon, not only for your inspiration, but also for responding to my email and accepting my request for you to write the foreword to this book as well as your grace, class, and generosity throughout the process.

Thank you to Mark Sanborn for your inspiration, stories, and lessons in leadership through your books and for giving me the opportunity earlier in my career to learn from you and represent you on stages, spreading Fred to audiences across the country. I wouldn't be an author and speaker today if not for your inspiration and encouragement back then.

Thank you to Larry Ross, my favorite professor at Florida Southern College, where I first began learning about the magic of the hospitality industry. You were more than a professor, and your gifts of teaching, inspiring, and encouragement have echoed in my heart and mind since I was a student in several of your classes.

Thank you to Michael Sturman, Linda Canina, Gary Thompson, Chekitan Dev, Bruce Tracey, Robert Kwortnik, and Tim Hinkin, my favorite graduate school professors at the Cornell Hotel School. My time at Cornell, diving even deeper into all things hospitality, was special and continues to drive me, inspire me, and compel me to give more of myself to be of service to others in as many ways as possible. Thank you for your service to our beloved hospitality industry over the years. You are all legends and heroes to those of us lucky enough to have been your students.

Thank you to my mentors and leaders in my roles in hospitality over the years, from Dave Chylinski, Scott Robinson, and Ralph Larsen to Scott Biedermann, Ellen Ruel, Dawn DeStefano, Jack Sharp, Jody Bainter, Stacy Ray, Will Farnsworth, Beth Neal, Trisha Warne, Ed Fouche, Randy Garfield, Tom McMahon, Jamie Papp, Steve Weitman, John Devlin, Jacob Lanning, Colleen Birch, Brian Gress, Todd Simons, Tom McCartney, Jeff Burge, Arthur Keith, Lisa Marchese, John Unwin, Anna Ulloa-Cantos, James T. Dawn, Derek DeSalvia, Ken Potrock, Karl Holz, Andy Berry, Steve Wilbanks, Annmarie El Haj, Lindsey Monje, April Stratton, Travis Cary, Amanda Marchese, Joshua Abad, Dave Wiley, Steve Gilmore, Julio Garneff, Amy Bishop, Cory Ferarro, and Dana Kuykendall. I've learned from each one of you, and I'm very grateful for the lessons in life and leadership.

APPENDIX:
MY HOSPITALITY JOURNEY

As I mentioned in the introduction, throughout my professional career, I've been blessed with opportunity after opportunity to work for and represent some of the most highly sought-after, game-changing brands in the world. I didn't always realize it at the time, but each career stop has in some way, shape, or form *positively changed the game* for people inside and outside their organizations.

Gaylord Palms Resort and Convention Center

The property opened in 2002 and completely disrupted the meeting, convention, and resort hotel space with its brand, legendary service, remarkable aesthetics, and inspirational corporate culture. Gaylord's first hotel opened in Nashville, Tennessee, in 1977. For the first time in twenty-five years, the company set out to change the game with a new, 1,406-room resort with four hundred thousand square feet of convention space in Orlando, Florida.

Opening shortly after September 11, 2001, when most hotels were cutting staff, downsizing, and suppressing innovation and growth,

Gaylord Palms held a grand-hire event that hosted thousands of prospective candidates, months prior to its opening.

I'm thankful they noticed and selected me. I'm also extremely proud of their success. Since opening Gaylord Palms, the company has expanded, opening Gaylord Texan in Grapevine, Texas, in 2004; Gaylord National in National Harbor, Maryland, near Washington, DC, in 2006; Gaylord Rockies in Aurora, Colorado, thirty minutes outside Denver in 2019; as well as Gaylord Bayfront in Chula Vista, California in 2021.

Gaylord Hotels and Resorts caught the attention of Marriott International, which bought the company in 2012 and operates all its properties today. Their success since that risky, game-changing resort hotel opened in 2002 is a result of their approach to leadership, culture, and service. I'm blessed to have had a front-row seat, and I'm proud now to share principles I learned from Gaylord Hotels with you in this book.

Disney's Pop Century Resort

Walt Disney World Resort enjoyed rapid, frequent, and consistent expansion with new hotels, theme parks, dining, and recreational amenities almost monthly since opening their magical doors in 1971.

In the fall of 2003, I was fortunate to have another front-row seat. Disney put together an all-star team of leaders from resorts, theme parks, and even their call centers. For the first time, the company went out on a limb and purposely chose leaders with vast experience in varying lines of business to open their newest, largest, and most complex resort yet. As they put it, "Drawing creativity from diversity."

Thankfully, I was noticed and selected to join the grand-opening team of the 2,880-room *Disney's Pop Century Resort*. I joined the front office leadership team as the only leader who came in as an external hire. I was blessed to work with and for a team of the most respected, celebrated, and successful Disney leaders the company ever assembled.

They taught me many transferable leadership principles and inspired me in the same ways I've set out to teach and inspire you on the pages of this book.

Encore at Wynn Las Vegas

In 1989, Steve Wynn assembled a team of visionaries and hotel operators that forever changed the skyline, culture, vibe, and overall *experience* of Las Vegas when they opened The Mirage. That same group *gave* us Treasure Island, Bellagio, and Wynn Las Vegas, all of which raised the *luxury-experience* and *guest-service* bar in Las Vegas and across the hospitality industry.

In 2008, even during the Great Recession, Mr. Wynn and his team raised the bar yet again. They built and opened Encore Las Vegas. I was invited to join Mr. Wynn and his team of executives to open the new, 2,034-room Encore at Wynn Las Vegas. I don't think I realized the magnitude of the experience. As years have passed, I feel blessed and grateful I was on that opening team. Encore at Wynn Las Vegas has been awarded the AAA Five Diamond Award every year since its opening. The Tower Suites at Encore and the Spa have both received the Forbes Travel Guide five-star award. Wynn and Encore collectively hold more five-star awards globally than any other casino resort. They're both considered two of the finest hotels in the world.

Since we opened Encore with the same gusto, bravado, and commitment to luxury service, many people from whom I learned valuable skills went on to open Encore at Wynn Macau in 2010, Wynn Palace on the Cotai Strip in 2016, and Encore Boston Harbor, which opened during the summer of 2019.

I'm proud to call these leaders my friends and former colleagues. I've shared principles and applications for becoming a better leader, which I learned from them.

The Cosmopolitan of Las Vegas

During the economic downturn in 2008 and 2009, two developers defaulted on a new build essentially on the fifty-yard line of the Las Vegas Strip due to financial concerns. Deutsche Bank, who was the largest lender in the project, decided to go all in. In 2010 they put an incremental $2 billion into the development, making The Cosmopolitan of Las Vegas, a $4-billion casino resort, which opened in arguably the worst economic time since the Great Depression of the 1930s.

Another all-star team was assembled with some of the brightest marketing minds, savvy casino hotel operators, culinary, culture, and brand curators, and disruptors the world had ever seen.

I was so grateful to have been noticed and selected to join that grand-opening team. From 2010 to 2014, I worked alongside some of the most dynamic business leaders of our time. I learned, listened, observed, and poured my heart and soul into changing the game in Las Vegas, as part of The Cosmopolitan community of CoStars. I'm so proud of what we created during that season, because many hotels, companies, and brands have since tried to emulate components of the brand, culture, and guest experience all for good reason.

Zappos, with arguably one of the most game-changing corporate cultures in the last century, meets regularly with executives and leaders with whom I worked at The Cosmopolitan. Their aim was to stay up with trends regarding what works and what doesn't work in today's modern workplace.

MGM Resorts, Caesars Entertainment, and others followed our lead as we pioneered an all-inclusive, loyalty marketing program where valued guests are rewarded for what they spend on gaming. Guests are also rewarded for resort, restaurant, retail, and entertainment spending.

In 2013, The Cosmopolitan was rated the best hotel in the world by Gogobot. It also was named to the Condé Nast Traveler Gold List as one of the top hotels in the world. Since the doors opened when many said we'd fail, the team has maintained some of the highest room rates, highest occupancy rates, the best restaurants, nightclubs, day clubs, and employee experiences the industry has ever seen.

The Cosmopolitan of Las Vegas was a game-changing opening in Las Vegas and a workplace culture disruptor for the business world. It also was a meaningful experience for me.

Disney Vacation Club

In 2014, I joined Disney Vacation Club, as the manager of sales for DVC's sales site at Disneyland Resort. I was a salesperson earlier in my career in travel-industry sales. Leading seasoned sales veterans and licensed Realtors in the vacation-ownership space was new, exciting, and challenging.

Disney is known for its full-length animated features, live action films that now include Marvel Studios and the Star Wars franchise. Of course, the Disney brand also includes its portfolio of global theme parks and resorts. While you may not be as familiar with Disney Vacation Club, their timeshare division, it's become an industry leader in experience, theming, accommodations, and of late, its exponential growth.

I joined the team when we opened a brand-new sales-and-preview center at the iconic Disneyland Resort. We opened and launched two new Disney Vacation Club Resorts, grew the size of our team by 30 percent, and implemented a new CRM system for the first time since DVC began twenty-five years prior.

I'm blessed and again thankful I was selected to lead the Disneyland team through a period of rapid growth and expansion, all while delivering pure Disney magic every day. Perhaps my most valuable lessons from this experience are also what makes Disney great; that's the ability to weave in *inspiration, experience,* and *storytelling* into everything we do as leaders, marketers, and people.

I hope the stories I shared from this impactful season of my career inspired you on your journey as well.

Corporate Training, Live Learning Experiences, and Consulting

In 2018, I launched the *Lead with Hospitality* message and platform with one purpose—to inspire leaders to create organizations where their teams feel *welcome, comfortable,* and *important.* I wrote and launched my first book, *Ballgames to Boardrooms: Leadership, Business, and Life Lessons From Our Coaches We Never Knew We Needed* in August of 2017. I wrote the book to connect with, inspire, and encourage up-and-comers in business and the corporate world who might feel stuck.

I've since been blessed and very grateful for opportunities to consult, speak to, and train teams and leaders in various businesses, hotels, and industries. I'm excited to share these same principles, illustrations, and applications you've read in this book.

Today, I'm able to do what I love—inspire people—because leaders, mentors, authors, speakers, and trainers inspired me. This book is a *thank-you* to the people, leaders, and brands who inspired me over the years. My intention was to simply lift you up so you're inspired to pass along the inspiration, encouragement, and leadership to people in your life—at work and at home.

I hope you enjoyed reading this book as much as I enjoyed writing it.

CONNECT WITH TAYLOR

If you are interested in contacting Taylor Scott and his team, visit www.LeadWithHospitality.com for more leadership development resources such as action plans, Taylor's weekly notes of encouragement, and live learning experiences: workshops, leadership coaching, and keynotes.

Phone: 321-297-6323
Email: info@leadwithhospitality.com
Online: www.LeadWithHospitality.com
Twitter: @tscott1502
Facebook: www.facebook.com/TaylorScottOfficial
Instagram: @tscott1502

Leadership Development: Virtual or In-Person Learning Experiences, Coaching, and Keynotes

All content is customizable to meet specific needs. Discover six learning experiences:

- Commitment to Connection
- Striving for Self-Mastery
- Leadership as a Service

- Purposeful Engagement for Leaders
- Coaching with Grace, Grit, and Intention
- Becoming Inspired to Inspire

Taylor's Lead with Hospitality platform, with proven principles on how to connect, strive for self-mastery, serve, engage, coach, and inspire has already been introduced and put into practice by several organizations and leaders of Fortune 500 companies.

Key Topics and Applications

Connect	Self-Mastery
• Science behind motivation and inspiration • How to connect in one-on-one meetings • How to prepare for and facilitate team meetings • How to stay connected through written communication	• Emotional intelligence (self-awareness, self-management, social awareness [empathy], relationship management) • Acceptance (accept yourself and your uniqueness, accept others for who they are, accept organizational realities) • Empathy (what empathy really means, how to put empathy into action, building trust by showing empathy)
Serve	**Engage**
• Servant leadership • Listening with empathy • Educating with feedback • Accountability: how to have tough coaching conversations • Delivering information, tools, and resources for your team	• Creating a sense of belonging • Genuine kindness as a leader • Power of purpose • Encouragement • Meaningful recognition

Coach	Inspire
• Grace and gracefulness as a leader • Creating the right environment • What really motivates people: competence, autonomy, and relatedness • Crafting a vision, setting SMART Goals, and creating action plans • Consistent communication as a coach • Celebrating wins and having accountability conversations	• The science behind inspiration and the art of delivering • How to feed your mind, body, and soul • The power of storytelling as a leader • Developing your leadership brand • Transforming jobs into meaningful work with experiences

NOTES

1. Chris Drysdale, Christina Chau, Todd Nordstrom, and Andrew Scarcella, "O. C. Tanner Institute 2020 Global Culture Report," Paragon Press, 2019, https://www.octanner.com/content/dam/oc-tanner/documents/white-papers/2019/INT-GCR2020-12.pdf.

2. Jim Harter, "Employee Engagement on the Rise in the U.S.," Gallup, August 26, 2018, news.gallup.com/poll/241649/employee-engagement-rise.aspx.

3. Thomas F. Mahan, Danny Nelms, Christopher Ryan Bearden, and Bratley Pearce, "2019 Retention Report," Work Institute, 2019, https://info.workinstitute.com/hubfs/2019%20Retention%20Report/Work%20Institute%202019%20Retention%20Report%20final-1.pdf.

4. Drysdale et al., "O. C. Tanner Institute 2020 Global Culture Report."

5. David Booth, *The Arts Go to School: Classroom-Based Activities That Focus on Music, Painting, Drama, Movement, Media, and More* (Portsmouth: Stenhouse Publishers, 2004).

6. Jonathan Haidt, *The Happiness Hypothesis: Putting Ancient Wisdom to the Test of Modern Science* (New York: Basic Books, 2006).

7. Mahan et al., "2019 Retention Report."

8. Dan Witters and Sangeeta Agrawal, "Well-Being Enhances Benefits of Employee Engagement," Gallup, October 27, 2015, www.gallup.com/workplace/236483/enhances-benefits-employee-engagement.aspx.

9. "New Cigna Study Reveals Loneliness at Epidemic Levels in America," Multivu, May 1, 2018, https://www.multivu.com/players/English/8294451-cigna-us-loneliness-survey/

10.   "About Kimpton: Award-Winning Boutique Hotels & Restaurants,"
       IHG, accessed August 11, 2020, www.ihg.com/kimptonhotels/content
       /us/en/press/kimpton-history.

11.   "Love Where You Work," IHG, accessed August 11, 2020, www.ihg
       .com/kimptonhotels/content/us/en/aboutus/careers (link inactive).

12.   Howard Beck, "Kerr and Draymond's Relationship Nearly Destroyed
       Warriors; Now It Fuels Them," Bleacher Report, May 24, 2018, bleacher
       report.com/articles/2777471-kerr-and-draymonds-relationship-nearly
       destroyed-warriors-now-it-fuels-them.

13.   "2020 State of Workplace Empathy," Businessolver, accessed August 6,
       2020, https://info.businessolver.com/en-us/empathy-2020-exec-summary.

14.   "2020 State of Workplace Empathy," Businessolver.

15.   Amy Gallo, "Why We Should Be Disagreeing More at Work," *Harvard
       Business Review*, January 3, 2018, hbr.org/2018/01/why-we-should-be
       -disagreeing-more-at-work.

16.   "2020 State of Workplace Empathy," Businessolver. Drysdale et al., "O.C.
       Tanner Institute 2020 Global Culture Report."

17.   Harry McCracken, "Satya Nadella on Learning, Listening, and His
       #1 Productivity Hack," Fast Company, November 8, 2019, www.fast
       company.com/90425588/satya-nadella-on-learning-listening-and-his
       -1productivity-hack.

18.   The American Institute of Stress, "Workplace Stress," accessed February
       20, 2020, www.stress.org/workplace-stress.

19.   Korn Ferry, "Workplace Stress Continues to Mount," accessed November
       14,2018,www.kornferry.com/insights/articles/workplace-stress-motivation.

20.   Francesca Gino, "The Business Case for Curiosity," *Harvard Business
       Review*, September-October 2018, hbr.org/2018/09/curiosity.

21.   Gino, "The Business Case for Curiosity."

22.   Bill George, Peter Sims, Andrew N. McLean, and Diana Mayer, "Dis-
       covering Your Authentic Leadership," *Harvard Business Review*, February
       2007, hbr.org/2007/02/discovering-your-authentic-leadership.

23.   "About Us," GiVE CULTURE, www.shopgiveculture.com/pages/our
       -why. Accessed August 10, 2020.

24. Craig Dowden, "Civility Matters! An Evidence-Based Review on How to Cultivate a Respectful Federal Public Service," Association of Professional Executives of the Public Service of Canada, May 15, 2015, apex.gc .ca/wp-content/uploads/2017/10/civility-report-eng.pdf.

25. Gina Vivinetto, "Emily Blunt Opens up about Childhood Stutter—and How She Overcame It," TODAY, April 6, 2018, www.today.com/pop culture/emily-blunt-opensabout-childhood-stutter-how-she-overcame -it-t126639.

26. "Interview: Sawubona," Global Oneness Project, accessed September 15, 2020, www.globalonenessproject.org/library/interviews/sawubona.

27. Bridget Edwards, "Namaste and Sawubona, a Zulu Greeting." Bridget-Edwards.com (blog), accessed September 14, 2019, bridget-edwards .com/namaste-and-sawubona-a-zulu-greeting/.

28. David Novak, "Recognizing Employees Is the Simplest Way to Improve Morale," Harvard Business Review, May 9, 2016, hbr.org/2016/05 /recognizing-employees-is-the-simplest-way-to-improve-morale.

29. The Build Network Staff, "Leadership: Say It Again. And Again. (And . . .)," Inc., February 18, 2014, www.inc.com/the-build-network/ leadership-say-it-again.html.

30. Ken Blanchard, Patricia Zigarmi, and Drea Zigarmi, Leadership and the One Minute Manager: A Situational Approach to Leading Others (New York: William Morrow, 2013).

31. "In Praise of Gratitude," Harvard Health Publishing, updated June 5, 2019, www.health.harvard.edu/newsletter_article/in-praise-of-gratitude.

32. Mark Sanborn, The Fred Factor: How Passion in Your Work and Life Can Turn the Ordinary into the Extraordinary (New York: Crown Publishing, 2004).

33. George T. Doran, "There's a S.M.A.R.T. way to write management's goals and objectives." Management Review (AMA FORUM) 70, no. 11 (November 1981): 35–36, community.mis.temple.edu/mis0855002 fall2015/files/2015/10/S.M.A.R.T-Way-Management-Review.pdf.

34. Ryan Pendell and Jim Harter, "10 Gallup Reports to Share With Your Leaders in 2019," Gallup, January 4, 2019, www.gallup.com/workplace /245786/gallup-reports-shareleaders-2019.aspx.

35. Scott Barry Kaufman, "Why Inspiration Matters," Harvard Business Review, November 8, 2011, hbr.org/2011/11/why-inspiration-matters.

36. Eric Garton and Michael Mankins, "Engaging Your Employees Is Good, but Don't Stop There," Harvard Business Review, December 9, 2015, hbr .org/2015/12/engaging-your-employees-is-good-but-dont-stop-there.

37. Kaufman, "Why Inspiration Matters."

38. Michael T. Bosworth and Ben Zoldan, *What Great Salespeople Do: The Science of Selling Through Emotional Connection and the Power of Story* (New York: McGraw-Hill Education, 2012).

39. "Association Releases 2019 State of the Restaurant Industry Report," National Restaurant Association, April 8, 2019, restaurant.org/Articles /News/Association-report-analyzes-industry-trends.

40. S. Lock, "Amusement and Theme Parks—Statistics & Facts," Statista, January 29, 2019, www.statista.com/topics/2805/amusement-and-theme -parks/.

41. Richard M. Ryan and Edward L. Deci, *Self-Determination Theory: Basic Psychological Needs in Motivation, Development, and Wellness* (New York: Guilford Publishing, 2017).

ABOUT THE AUTHOR

Photo by Jenna Joseph

TAYLOR SCOTT is an inspirational keynote speaker, thought leader for up-and-comers starting out on their leadership journeys, and a leadership-development consultant. Through his books, workshops, keynotes, and one-on-one coaching, he inspires audiences and consults frontline supervisors and leaders of leaders in Fortune 500 companies and lifestyle brands nationwide to become their best, deliver their best, and experience the best life possible.

Taylor leverages his personal experiences and twenty years working in the hospitality industry for Disney Parks and Resorts, Gaylord Hotels and Resorts, Wynn Resorts, and The Cosmopolitan of Las Vegas to connect with and inspire leaders on the front lines in various lines of business.

He has delivered a number of keynotes and leadership-development workshops since 2011 for colleges, universities, school systems, and Fortune 500 companies in corporate America. His energy, enthusiasm, and engaging style of storytelling leave audiences feeling inspired, encouraged, and ready to give their best.

Taylor is the bestselling author of *Ballgames to Boardrooms* and *Lead with Hospitality*.

He earned a bachelor of science in business administration from Florida Southern College in Lakeland, Florida, and a master's in management of hospitality from Cornell University's School of Hotel Management in Ithaca, New York. He lives in Las Vegas, Nevada, with his wife, Jenna.